Declination

The Other Dimension

Kt Boehrer

Kt Boehrer was a long-time member and supporter of the American Federation of Astrologers. Prior to her death in 2004, she expressed her desire that the American Federation of Astrologers publish and keep Declination in print. Anyone who is a relation of Kt is invited to contact AFA so that the organization's records can be updated.

ISBN-13: 978-0-86690-669-2

Cover Design: Jack Cipolla

Published by:
American Federation of Astrologers, Inc.
6535 S. Rural Road
Tempe, AZ 85283

Contents

Introduction

Two things seem certain. One, astrology does not give up its secrets without a struggle, and two, astrology tends to reward the struggle generously on the tangent.

The goal of this struggle has always been focused very narrowly on a single method of obtaining revealing and specific information from the hitherto silent voice of declination. On the curve, in a manner of speaking, there have been surprises and rewards in the form of totally unrelated insight.

For this reason, the reader will find several aids to rectification and delineation that are not related to declination but have proven their value in the course of this research.

In view of the considerable number of requests for all previously published material on the subject of declination, several articles originally written for *Stellium Quarterly* are included in this book.

Consequently, there is some repetition of material between the earlier articles and the more recent material, possibly regrettable but definitely unavoidable.

There is some repetition, even in the newer material, that is not necessarily a bad thing in as much as repetition is a positive aid to memory. However, that is not its *raison d'etre*; it just seemed unavoidable given the nature of the exercise.

The concept of decoding delineation is very simple and the means appear quite clearly the only way in which to achieve the goal of specificity in delineation. However the potential for complexity (and possibly occasional confusion) is conspicuous and sometimes avoided only by careful and tedious attention to detail.

Finally, the research, rules, theories and techniques presented here have been developed within the limits of accepted astrological law. There is no speculative character to this material, every step of the rationale is strongly conservative and soundly supported by much used and traditional rules of the science.

Kt Boehrer

Chapter 1

Lost and Found

There is an aspect that has long been known by man and long forgotten by astrology.

The Lost Aspect

The lost aspect exists today only in the form of a hand signal. Its current use is one of great spirituality. Because of this the world is largely unaware of its astrological association and origin.

Over time it has become completely disassociated from astrology and has been grafted onto a different philosophy altogether. We see its symbol used in daily life, seen in the media and constantly in use in certain groups and gatherings.

It is documented in ancient art, history, and religion, both oriental and occidental, and early depictions of this rare and powerful aspect appear in certain ancient Buddhist images and artifacts from as early as 600 B.C. Later it is found incorporated into the design of Byzantine icons that were in great demand circa 100 to 400 A.D. The influence of Byzantium was widespread throughout the Mediterranean world and northern Europe, and Buddhism was known throughout the eastern and oriental world, India and China. Therefore, the World and his wife knew then and know now this aspect and its symbol, and many love it well for then as now they recognized the great blessing it conveys.

From the time of the Dark Ages, and even into the 20th century, the symbol of this aspect has been used to ward off the Evil Eye, to protect against evil, to prevail against the enemy. It had the power to make strong men tremble. It was said that the good need not fear it for evil flees before it. It was particularly comforting to people of all classes in Europe and even the New World during the more than thousand years following the Dark Ages that commenced about 500 A.D. Even so, the literature and social history of the 19th and 20th centuries reveal that its use may have lessened to a certain extent during that time but that it did not die. Indeed, there has even been a resurgence of faith in the power and strength of this aspect and its symbol in the 20th century and its use will continue into the 21st century.

Where did it come from? How do we know it was associated with astrology?

Steeped in history, mysticism, spirituality and the mists of time, its origin shines with magnificent clarity once you have eyes to see, for this aspect is symbolized by the angle of the forefinger and middle finger of Christ on Byzantine icons and by the angle of the forefinger and middle finger of certain Buddhist statues and by the angle of the forefinger and middle finger of the pope when he gives his blessing and clearly conveys God's blessing of peace, protection, and love on his children. The angle of the forefinger and middle finger measures 23.5 degrees.

And long before Buddhism and Christianity, witchcraft and satanism it was the holy measure of the 23.5 degree angle of earth's axis, the inclination of the ecliptic over the equator, a milestone of major proportions in man's material and spiritual, mental and emotional understanding of the Universe, a benchmark of progress and a blessing for us all.

The Found Aspect

Natal planetary declination describes conditions and impressions or influences in life that were not obvious or easily identified prior to March 1975, when the first issue of *Stellium Quarterly* was published for the principal purpose of presenting this study of declination to the public.

The work began with the out-of-bounds planets—out of bounds because they had achieved a declination greater than the maximum declination of the ecliptic and the realization that longitude provided no information about the unusual behavior of these planets. In fact, their remarkable condition is masked and/or concealed by their longitude. Such planets and asteroids reflect and define the eccentricity of their orbits by their declination. Their orbits are eccentric even while within the maximum declination of the ecliptic but are not beyond the realm of reason until they go beyond the maximum ecliptic limits (23N/S28). Because their aspects are not totally identified by longitude their complete influence must be determined through information encoded in their declination and the aspects that declination may reveal when related to longitude.

The planets that exhibit markedly eccentric orbits are the Moon, Mercury, Venus, Mars, and Pluto. Ceres, Pallas, Juno, Vesta and other asteroids may also exhibit eccentric orbits, and therefore at certain times fulfilling the requirements of the astronomical aspect called the "anomaly" or the "anomalous aspect," hitherto unknown in astrology.

The Rule for Identification of the Anomaly

1. The astronomical definition of the anomalous aspect relates to the distance of a planet from its perihelion, the angle measuring apparent irregularities in the motion (orbit) of a planet or asteroid. (A dictionary further defines the anomaly as "deviation from the general rule, method or analogy; irregular, peculiar, abnormal, inconstant with the normal.")

This introduces some very interesting considerations. A planet, for example, does not suddenly develop an eccentric orbit when it reaches the maximum ecliptic declination. In fact, planetary orbits may be slightly eccentric while within the maximum declination of the ecliptic, and during that slightly eccentric orbit they may never exceed the maximum ecliptic declination.

Example: If the Moon is in 1 Aries 00, 0N24 (the Sun's degree of declination when at 1 Aries 00), it is not in an eccentric orbit. If the Moon is at longitude 1 Aries 00, declination 3N46, the Moon's orbit is slightly eccentric and it may be making one or more anomalous aspects that can be identified only through determining the longitudinal sign, degree, and minute occupied by the Sun when in declination 3N46. By reference to the Declination/Longitude Conversion Table we see that the Sun at declination 3N46 is always within a few minutes of 9 Aries 15. Thus we know that the Moon is openly and normally engaged in making aspects from and receiving aspects at 1 Aries 00 but that, under cover of declination, it is making anomalous aspects from and receiving anomalous aspects at 9 Aries 15. This is clearly aberrant or unusual behavior, irregular, peculiar, secret and sometimes abnormal, illegal, unacceptable or beyond the call of duty or responsibility.

Of all the lights and planets, the Moon changes declination most rapidly in harmony with the speed with which she progresses longitudinally through the chart, serving us as a scanning device, our personal radar, checking all natal positions as well as the progression of our affairs as our lives proceed, always returning on a monthly basis to her natal longitudinal base but *not* necessarily simultaneously to her natal declination therefore not always totally dependable in her assessment of the state of our affairs.

In watching the Moon on a daily basis we are watching her longitudinal transits over a period of approximately twenty-eight days; but we must also watch her progression by both longitude and declination through the years as she returns by longitudinal progression approximately every twenty-eight days (by transit) or twenty-eight years (by progression, one day equals one year) to assess the state of her affairs. Her longitudinal return is dependable, but her return by declination is a sometime thing that does not necessarily coincide with her longitudinal return. In fact, in certain instances the progressed Moon may never return to her natal declination again throughout the entire course of the lifetime. If the native happens to have been born in the last orbit of the Moon's out-of-bounds cycle it will be approximately ten years before her erratic cycle may take her out-of-bounds again and as a result she can never by progression throughout the course of the native's life attain the declination that she occupied at birth.

It is equally important to observe that those people born during the lunar out-of-bounds cycle will undergo periods of change (sometimes disruptive) about every twelve to fourteen years when the progressed Moon goes out of bounds. If the natal Moon is not out-of-bounds at birth but goes out-of-bounds three days later, age three will then introduce the first disruptive year of life and this will continue to occur every twelve to fourteen years (twelve to fourteen days) for the rest of their life or until the Moon completes her out-of-bounds cycle. How long this lasts depends entirely on where the Moon is in her out-of-bounds cycle at the time of birth.

The Moon's aspects and the aspects of any planet or asteroid while in an eccentric cycle will include anomalous aspects, whether traveling inside or outside the ecliptic limit 23N/S28 and these aspects are identified only by declination. The further the planet's declination is removed from the declination of the Sun when in the degree and minute of longitude occupied by the planet, the more extreme is the planet's orbit.

Basic Rules for the Use of Declination

Rule 1. There is only one celestial body in every chart that is always found in the true degree of declination corresponding to its longitudinal position by sign and degree along the ecliptic.

That remarkable planet (light) is the Sun, which sets the angle of declination while apparently traversing through space and marking the exact spot where its position by longitudinal sign and degree intersect its true declination along the ecliptic, and therefore never in a position to make an anomalous aspect.

Rule 2. All earthly events occur along the ecliptic; therefore, the declination of the longitudinal position of all planets must be found by reference to the declination of the Sun when located in the longitudinal degree and sign in which the planet is found.

Rule 3. Planets and asteroids are often found in a degree of declination that is far from the Sun's longitudinal position along the ecliptic when found in the degree of declination occupied by the planet. In such a case the given declination of the planet must be located in the true sign and degree of longitude along the ecliptic as set by the Sun when in that degree of declination. When there is a marked difference in the declination of the planet and the declination of the Sun when in the same sign and degree of longitude, the planet is in an eccentric orbit and making anomalous aspects.

> Example: Moon at 17 Taurus 18, 14N29. The Sun at 14N29 occupies a longitudinal position at 8 Taurus 57 and/or a position at 21 Leo 03, which will always be the true position on the ecliptic of any planet at 14N29 declination. Therefore, any planet in that degree of declination and a markedly different longitudinal position is in an eccentric orbit and will make anomalous aspects.

Rule 4. The Moon at 17 Taurus 18 will also indicate a declination of 16N55 (the Sun's declination when found at 17 Taurus 18). A planet or asteroid with a very eccentric orbit may be found in a longitudinal aspect to our example Moon at 17 Taurus 18, while throwing parallels to planets in very different longitudinal signs and degrees due to its declination. This may be of marked importance in understanding conditions and forecasting events.

Example: Pluto at 17 Scorpio 18 opposed our example Moon (above) at 17 Taurus 18. This is a traditional aspect and easily identified. However, something very important and not readily observed is also happening. Pluto, due to its eccentric orbit, is found by declination at 2S56, which is the Sun's declination when found at 7 Libra 22, and from this position of influence may make aspects to planets at 7 degrees of almost any sign.

Rule 5. Planets found at a declination that exceeds the maximum declination of the Sun at 23N/S28 declination are called out of bounds. These planets can only make anomalous aspects and these anomalous aspects can only be identified by determining their declination angle to the ecliptic as exemplified here and by finding the equivalent sign, degree and minute of the Sun when in the corrected degree and minute of declination occupied by the out-of-bounds planet.

Example: Ceres (the legal wife, the maternal principal) at 0 Aquarius 53, 31S16.

Problem: to bring Ceres by correction of its out-of-bounds declination to its ecliptic declination and its corresponding sign and degree in longitude.

Ceres 31 S 16 declination

minus <u>23 S 28</u> maximum ecliptic declination

minus <u>7 : 48</u> difference from maximum ecliptic

equals 15 S 40 declination related to the ecliptic

The Sun when found at 15S40 is in 13 Aquarius 13 with its co-declination at 16 Scorpio 47. Therefore, Ceres, out of bounds at 31S16 declination, when corrected for its angle to the ecliptic makes anomalous aspects from its declination position at 13 Aquarius 13 and 16 Scorpio 47 and receives aspects at those anomalous longitudinal positions.

The true declination of Ceres when located at 0 Aquarius 53 is determined by reference to the Declination/Longitude Conversion Table, where we find that 0 Aquarius 53 on the ecliptic is found at declination 19S42.

It is extremely important to identify the anomalous position of a natal planet and the anomalous aspects it may be making in a natal chart. It is equally important to trace the anomalous aspects made by a progressed or transiting planet in an eccentric orbit to planetary positions in the natal chart. These aspects are identifiable only through their declination converted to longitudinal positions.

Chapter 2

The Cosmic Information Super Highway

It is not surprising that nothing has been heard in the last thousand years or so about how to understand and use declination in the practice of astrology because it is a very complex subject that must be carefully studied in order to apply it as a viable technique.

Super Highway of The Universe

The conditions and terminology of declination are virtually unknown because the astrological tradition for at least a thousand years has dismissed the subject of declination and the parallel aspect with such a paucity of information as to make it possible to record the entire body of inherited knowledge in a brief paragraph.

In short, the parallel is the strongest of all aspects, it is formed by declination, and it is of the nature of a longitudinal conjunction or opposition. It frequently occurs at the time of a conjunction (longitudinal), thus giving added importance to the conjunction and some kind of twist or quirk to the aspect. The influence of the parallel is considered to last longer than that of a longitudinal conjunction or opposition.

Unfortunately, we have for a long time been unable to apply declination to delineation or delineation to declination in any but the most simplistic fashion because we speak nothing but longitude (the mother tongue of astrology).

When this research into the mystery that is declination was begun in 1973 it was obvious that declination carried more import than simple timing. Clearly there were hints and indications of considerable importance to the understanding of character, life conditions, and events of an extraordinary nature and it was equally plain to be seen that the only option available for research lay in finding a way to translate declination into the language of astrology, into longitudinal terminology.

For this to happen, a link between longitude and declination had to be established, a way to bridge the gap, to relate these two measurements, a means by which these two celestial measurements could be associated. There were only two available options: either the celestial equator or the ecliptic. Although declination is measured by a series of parallels to the equator, there appeared to be no way to draw meaningful information from these measurements because while declination is measured from the equator, the longitudinal signs of the zodiac form an arc that crosses the equator at two points only and exists principally in an arc that falls on either side of the equator.

The Royal Highway of the Sun, where, we are told, all earthly events occur, turned out to be the rainbow leading to a pot of gold, the yellow brick road that provides another dimension in astrology, the information cosmic super highway of the Sun and our Universe where declination and longitude meet and travel instructions are provided.

The correlation of degrees and minutes of declination with degrees and minutes of longitude along the ecliptic is the open door to another dimension. Previously hidden aspects of great importance will be revealed and a more comprehensive and profound understanding of the natal chart will be achieved.

Cycles and Psychological Patterns
of the Out-of-Bounds Planets

What do you do with an out-of-bounds planet?

The answer is simple: you do a lot of research. Find out all about declination and how it might be related (in some hitherto unrecognized fashion) to longitude and the ecliptic. Either find or create a language for declination. Study the declination of planets as they transit through longitude and declination. Look at their orbits over a considerable period of time. In short, learn everything possible about the movement of planets through the zodiac and through space.

The research started with the natal charts of hundreds of famous people born with out-of-bounds planets whose lives were more or less open books because of their successes and careers or their failures in career or personal lives.

The next step was the inclusion of hundreds of clients' charts with natal out-of-bounds planets and specific dates for major events in their lives.

Concurrent with this, a program of reading every available word that had been written about planetary declination, planetary orbits, and the ecliptic was begun and expanded to include astronomy and related sciences.

The second phase of this research led to a much greater understanding of the Universe and to a practical and scientific understanding of why and how astrology works.

As a result, the research sorted itself into two categories. One category is the declination/codeclination positions, i.e., the degree and minute of longitude with which each degree and minute of declination is associated. The second category was concentrated on the influence of a planet when it is out of bounds or beyond the ecliptic limit of 23N/S28 as determined by the apparent movement of the Sun.

The second area of research is simplicity itself. Out-of bounds-planets may be recognized at sight and by the simple fact that they are found beyond the ecliptic limit. It is possible to give them the keywords "beyond normal conditions or expectations." Their influence is usually easily understood within the context of the chart by reference to traditional information.

For example, the Moon commonly relates to emotions, family, home, mother, and the maternal principal. Therefore, the Moon out of bounds will indicate conditions related to the emotions, family, home, mother, and maternal Instincts that are unusual, beyond normal expectations and/or conditions.

Out-of-bounds planets are easily recognized by their reported declination by computer or ephemeris. It is rarely necessary to calculate their exact declination; in fact, only the Moon moves fast enough to require calculation for placement in the natal chart and in horary charts and events charts in which continuing activity over a period of time is important.

The only mathematical adjustment relating to the out-of-bounds planets is the following simple procedure:

Moon out of bounds at 27N45 must be related to the ecliptic in order to determine its declination point and its corresponding longitude along the ecliptic that will react to transits from planets whose declination is no greater than 23N/S28. The Moon's corrected or adjusted declination will then provide a degree of longitude on the ecliptic and its corresponding solstice point that will respond to progressions and transits.

Example: O-O-B Moon 27N45
minus   -23N28 maximum ecliptic
result   - 4 :17 must be subtracted from
maximum ecliptic   23N28
result   19N11 planetary co-declination
Moon 19N11 = 25 Taurus 44; solstice point is 4 Leo 16.

The Moon's co-declination can be located on the ecliptic by reference to the Declination/Longitude Conversion Table in this book.

The out-of-bounds condition is cyclical in nature, the cycle varying naturally with the speed of movement of the planet involved. In a typical lunar cycle we find that the Moon remains within the ecliptic limits for an average of nine years, never once during this period venturing beyond the maximum 23N/S28 ecliptic declination. This within bounds period alternates with a ten-year period or cycle during which the Moon achieves out-of-bounds status for a period of about two to two and a half days every ten to fourteen days.

Venus usually goes out of bounds twice a year, although in some years she may exceed 23N/S28 declination only once while other years can find her out of bounds as many as three times. Her out-of-bounds periods can range from as little as one day to as many as 56 to 60 days, while her within bounds period can last for as much as a year (example, January 1897 through December 1897). Only the Moon and Venus can reach the 28N/S00 declination in their out-of-bounds journey.

Mercury achieves out-of-bounds status two or three times a year with occasional intervals in which this condition occurs only once in a year. The out-of-bounds condition exists for a widely fluctuating period of time, varying from as little as one or two days to as much as a month.

The heavier and slower the planet, the less frequent the out-of-bounds cycle and the longer the out-of-bounds cycle endures. For example, Mars normally goes out of bounds only once a year and can maintain this out-of-bounds condition for two to two and a half months at a time. Mercury and Mars never exceed 27N/S00 declination in their out-of-bounds cycle.

Jupiter and Uranus rarely exceed the 23N/S28 ecliptic limit and then only by minutes. Jupiter goes out of bounds about every six years, and once out of bounds, maintains out-of-bounds status for a period of approximately six to nine weeks. Uranus goes out of bounds approximately every 49 years, remaining outside the ecliptic much of the time for the next four-year period.

Saturn maintains fairly close contact with the ecliptic yet never moves beyond 23N/S28 declination, thus never breaching the ring, or boundary, of normality for our universe. Saturn, as the planet of discipline, hard work, and testing, I feel, is inclined to strict adherence to normal limitations and is all-important in establishing reality for our world.

Neptune is the only other planet that, as far as I have been able to determine, never exceeds the maximum ecliptic limits, a fact for which we should be very grateful since Neptune is the planet that rules illusion, a failure to recognize reality.

Pluto's orbit is extremely eccentric. Many astrologers have remarked on the fact that you never know when Pluto is going to deal a sharp blow, a matter that is hard to understand because Pluto is the heaviest, slowest moving of all the planets and we always know where it is by longitude. Of course the secret is in the extremity of Pluto's orbit. It is sometimes in a degree of declination that intersects the ecliptic so far from its longitudinal position that it is impossible to recognize the aspect that activates it or anticipate the timing of its action/reaction unless its declination has been converted to longitude. Like the other heavy planets, when it goes out of bounds it remains out of bounds off and on for many years at a time. For example, Pluto went out of bounds in about 1939 and remained out of bounds for a long period of time on an intermittent basis, into the early 1950s. The declination cycle and influence of Pluto, like everything else about that enigmatic planet, deserves serious individual study.

The Sun, life giver of our planet, and not properly a planet at all, sets the ecliptic limits for the normal state of affairs for our Universe.

One further point of interest: the Moon may never go out of bounds when in the signs of Aries, Libra, Virgo, or Pisces. It can and does go out of bounds in Taurus-Scorpio, Gemini-Sagittarius, Cancer-Capricorn, and Leo -Aquarius.

As interesting as the statistics on out-of-bounds planetary behavior may be, the delineation patterns that began to emerge from the research were even more fascinating. Let us begin to examine the influence of the planets and the patterns of their behavior.

A natal out-of-bounds Moon is associated with orphaning or some alienation from the mother. As research progressed it became more and more indicative of some degree of child abuse on either a mental, emotional, or physical level. These people may well be considered the step-children—the Cinderellas of the zodiac (regardless of their sex). The native may be orphaned by either the death of a parent or parents, or abandonment by one or both parents. In any event, the final result and most damaging aspect is the deprivation of the mother's love and care for reasons of death, ill health, economic necessity, or desertion. Occasionally the mother is so harsh and dictatorial, uncaring and critical, so obviously resentful of her inability to shunt responsibility for the child onto someone else that the relationship is extremely hostile.

There seems to be a compensatory factor at work for these people (the out-of-bounds Moon natives) for most often they achieve success, recognition, and wealth. Indeed, enough of them become wealthy for us to consider the out-of-bounds Moon natives, generally speaking, as the millionaires of the zodiac. Rejection in early life creates some emotional insecurity that they strive to overcome by proving their worth to the world. The lack of good mother-child relations apparently engenders a basic insecurity that drives these people to a high achievement level in their search for love, respect, influence, and security. In many cases, long after mother is dead and gone, that mother's child, born with an out-of-bounds Moon, is still striving to achieve something that will allow him or her to say, "Mom would be proud of me."

The out-of-bounds Moon occupying a critical position in the natal chart or involved in critical aspects can indicate a serious weight problem.

The out-of-bounds Moon in the female chart frequently indicates many children unless (and sometimes in spite of) a positive and determined effort to practice birth control is undertaken. Even so, the out-of-bounds Moon female will usually have at least one child and this child is often unplanned and unwanted.

In such cases we often find the out-of-bounds Moon mother both critical and demanding. The relationship with the child or children is usually difficult, the child being troublesome in some way, possibly rebellious or disobedient; the mother is often disappointed, feeling that the child is too frivolous and does not apply himself or herself to work, to the acquisition of wealth (or at least to the making and saving of money); to achieving a position of security and respect. The insecurity of the mother is transferred to the child. This pattern is sometimes observable through a number of generations and occasionally seems to be a self-perpetuating condition.

On the other hand, we find that the male born with Moon out of bounds often does not have children although he usually suffers an intense longing for them. If he is fortunate enough to have a child, it may not long survive, especially if it is of the male sex. If it does survive, the child may be sickly or sometimes effeminate in nature. These out-of-bounds Moon men frequently adopt children, seeming to prefer daughters and often become doting, indulgent, gentle, adoring stepfathers.

An important variation from this influence is found when two out-of-bounds Moon people marry as in the case of Princess Margaret and her former husband Anthony Armstrong Jones, both born with Moon out of bounds. A moment's reflection will demonstrate the out-of-bounds Moon's influence in these two lives. During her childhood, the world was regaled with stories of Princess Margaret's childish attempts to gain the same kind of love and attention that her sister Elizabeth automatically was accorded by virtue of being heiress to the throne of Great Britain. Anthony Armstrong Jones was the victim of divorced parents and subsequent step-parents and, according to published reports, did not have the opportunity to enjoy a normally close and constant mother-son relationship. His rise from obscurity to fame, wealth, prestige, and security as the husband of Princess Margaret demonstrates the fairy tale quality of the rags to riches out-of-bounds Moon. Princess Margaret also experienced a similar but less extreme change when she suddenly became second in line to the British throne.

When two out-of-bounds Moon people marry, as in this case, they usually have no trouble in producing healthy children; this appears to be the only major deviation from the individual Moon out-of-bounds pattern.

We also note that this marriage of two out-of-bounds Moon people was a stormy affair and speculate that both were extremely insecure, each suffering from a great need to find a place to be first in their relationship and in their social group and thus were drawn into an extremely competitive relationship, each demanding of the other some response of love and emotion that each was unable to provide.

Two charts that come instantly to mind as most descriptive of the natal out-of-bounds Moon are those of Queen Victoria of England and Babe Ruth, the American Sultan of Swat.

Those of you who are familiar with the story of Queen Victoria's life will have already recognized the out-of-bounds Moon pattern as it applies to her. The Cinderella aspect of her sudden elevation to heiress to the throne, the death of her father when she was only a few months old—a death, incidentally, that left her at the mercy of her mother, a very dictatorial, unloving and unlovable woman who kept Victoria virtually a prisoner until the day she succeeded to the throne. Until that day Victoria had literally never had a moment's solitude, even being required to share her sleeping quarters with her mother or governess. On the very day that Victoria became queen she retired her mother from her presence and from that moment in time maintained a considerable distance from her both physically and emotionally.

Victoria married and gave birth to a large family of children, some of whom displeased her quite seriously and all of whom feared her inordinately—a fear that carried over for two generations. After the first flush of youth Victoria suffered from an increasingly serious weight problem, becoming quite obese.

Rising from virtual poverty and obscurity, Victoria attained success, distinction and recognition, at the same time increasing her wealth beyond the measure normally meted out even to an empress. It was Victoria who laid the foundation for the great personal fortune that her descendants enjoy to this very day. She dictated manners and morals to the entire western world over a period of nearly a century, for her influence survived long after her death. Indeed, the Victorian period survives even today as one of the most strongly defined and distinctive periods in the history of the world.

Babe Ruth is typical of the out-of-bounds Moon male. The oldest of eight children, of whom only he and one other survived, he was reared in poverty and misery. His father, a tough, short-tempered man, ran a tavern in a grim part of Baltimore. His mother worked long hours in the tavern and was ill, tired and worn out by life, having no strength left over for the care of her children. The Babe said later that he had never known family life. By age seven he had been on the streets for three or four years and was involved with a tough street gang. Warned by police that he was headed for trouble, his parents placed him in St. Mary's Industrial School, a home for orphans, street urchins and boys who were in trouble with the law; he was to know no other home for the next twelve years. It was here that he learned to play baseball and from this grim and poverty-stricken background his drive, determination and ambition to achieve success and security took him to the top in the baseball world and made him a wealthy man. He became a hero in the eyes of the American public, one of the best loved of all American sports figures. From potential criminal he came to be known as the Prince of Pounders, the King of Clout, the Sultan of Swat—the greatest drawing card in the history of baseball!

Throughout his life he loved children, going out of his way to help them both personally and through the Babe Ruth Foundation, which he established to help needy children get an education through scholarships. His love for children was so great that he undertook to change his personal lifestyle when he realized that his wild ways were setting a bad example for children all over the United States. Because he and his wife were unable to have children, they adopted a girl named Dorothy. Later, after the death of his first wife, he married again, this time a beautiful widow with a daughter. Together with Claire, his second wife, her daughter Julie, and Dorothy, his own adopted daughter, the Babe established a sound and happy home and family.

During his entire baseball career the Babe had a continuing problem with his weight which frequently ballooned to more than 225 pounds. Contemporary psychiatrists and psychologists would equate this weight problem and his gargantuan appetite with the insecurity fostered by being an unwanted child. In fact, the Babe made it plain throughout his life that being unwanted haunted him even at the peak of his career and great success.

It must be confessed at this point that when Babe Ruth was chosen to illustrate the male Moon out-of-bounds pattern, I knew only that he was reared in an orphanage, came from a poor family, had no children of his own, and achieved fame and wealth. In doing the necessary research to verify these points it became surprisingly and abundantly clear that his life pattern fit the pattern in all particulars, in every precise detail. Even astrologers are amazed by the accuracy of astrology!

A word of caution: natives with the Moon and one or more of the other planets out of bounds will not fit this out-of-bounds Moon pattern. Combinations of out-of-bounds planets produce some extremely interesting types. For example, August Rodin, the great sculptor, was born with the Moon, Mercury, and Venus out-of-bounds. Ivan the Terrible, brutal Russian czar, had Uranus and Pluto out of bounds, Thomas Becket, martyred Archbishop of Canterbury, was born when Mercury and Jupiter were out of bounds. Many musicians have Mars out of bounds—usually accompanied by one or two other out-of-bounds planets. Berlioz and Brahms both had Venus and Mars out of bounds. Beethoven had Mercury and Mars out-of-bounds. William Shakespeare's natal chart includes Venus and Mars out of bounds. In fact, so many members of the arts (including the performing arts) are found with Venus-Mars or Mercury-Mars out of bounds that we lean to the theory that these combinations produce considerable talent in some artistic field.

Richard the Third, much vilified king of England, was born with Venus and Pluto out of bounds, and Plato, venerable Greek philosopher, was born with the Moon, Mars and Pluto out of bounds, the latter at a remarkable extreme of 31S04.

Theoretically, as many as six planets (Mercury, Venus, Mars, Jupiter, Uranus, and Pluto) and the Moon may be simultaneously out of bounds. In fact, more than three out-of-bounds planets at any given moment in time would be extremely unusual.

It is not easy to find a wide selection of charts with only Mercury out of bounds. Those that have come to our attention indicate that the out-of-bounds Mercury may be associated with considerable imagination, great curiosity, and a talent for the acquisition of knowledge. It is sometimes indicative of an ability to master more than one language as well as a gift for mimicry in some cases. On the negative side a speech problem can be present and the native can be very shy and sometimes nervous, self-conscious.

Venus out of bounds can indicate talent, creativity and romanticism in addition to a marked tendency to an overwhelming love and complete devotion for a person, cause, or pursuit. They might love, not too wisely but too well.

An out-of-bounds Mars is a fighter—daring, energetic, courageous, venturesome, often attracted to a career that is associated with an element of danger. The negative side may show in furious temper, anger, and/or violence.

Out-of-bounds Jupiter frequently brings typical Jupiterian luck and blessings and beauty, but the native is often somewhat spoiled by all this good fortune.

Uranus out of bounds often indicates an inventive, innovative nature with a tendency toward eccentricity. It can be associated with an impersonal, ruthless attitude and is frequently found in the charts of assassins or would-be assassins. Interesting examples of the out-of-bounds Uranus are found in the charts of Howard Hughes and Aristotle Onassis. Another less typical and much more pleasant example is Cary Grant, who was an exceedingly witty, intelligent and talented man and just a touch eccentric in a rather delightful fashion.

Pluto out of bounds is difficult to define in a personal sense because most individuals born during its average fifteen-year out-of-bounds period will have only Pluto out of bounds.

James Boehrer, in an article written for *Stellium Quarterly* in 1983, noted that Pluto is the planet that rules personal behavior. He may well have provided the best clue to the influence of the out-of-bounds Pluto. Certainly the children born in the late 1940s and early 1950s were the group who first introduced the generation gap of the 1960s and 1970s. This generation gap was widely attributed to a lack of communication or poor communication with earlier generations. This theory was widely promoted but its validity was questionable. The real problem was a matter of personal behavior and a total inability of the different generations to understand each others' personal value systems, life styles and behavior patterns.

It became more and more apparent during the course of this research that, while out-of-bounds planets make their mark on the character, personality, and sometimes the physical body, more importantly they appear to establish a paradigm or archetype for life. It also became more and more obvious that of all the out-of-bounds influences, that of the Moon is the most dependable and important.

We have examined the lunar archetype in this chapter and would only add that the extent to which the features of this pattern are manifested may vary, dependent on other indications in the chart. Currently, we find many severely abused children whose charts exemplify the most extreme examples of what I have chosen to call the lunar paradigm, and it should be understood that the lunar paradigm is the most specifically definitive of all the planetary patterns.

This is due to the nature and influence of the Moon. Moving rapidly (twelve to sixteen degrees of longitude per twenty-four hours with a corresponding speed of movement through declination), it emphasizes and illuminates the Moon's major role as ruler of intuition, sensitivity, awareness, and watchfulness; a personal radar that constantly scans every chart placement very quickly and very frequently. Its speed of movement is responsible for the sudden manifestation of crises in the lite and we understand that the severity of a crisis depends on the degree of emotional reaction triggered by the event.

The Moon in its travel makes obvious longitudinal aspects. Its parallels of declination are basically ignored when in fact they are triggering aspects that are most important, particularly at times of crisis. It is not enough to identify those aspects by declination alone; that declination needs to be related to both longitude and the ecliptic. This is accomplished by identifying the natal declination and co-declination of all the planets in the chart (and any asteroids that are customarily used), which then allows the astrologer to examine all the visible and invisible aspects that the Moon is making as it constantly scans our personal schematic or genetic pattern.

The planetary paradigms of the out-of-bounds planets Mercury, Venus, Mars, and Jupiter are less specifically defined due to their slower movement through longitude and declination thus indicating conditions and or characteristics that are basic to the individual and are less susceptible to identification because their influence is so much a part of the native and his life that they are taken for granted unless associated with a particular position in the chart. Even so, the outlines of the life pattern will not have the clarity of the lunar paradigm.

The heavy, slow-moving planets that may be found out of bounds are Uranus and Pluto. Their influence on the life pattern is associated principally with those social/political/scientific patterns that influence the generations, although Uranus out of bounds is typically related to remarkable changes that may take place in the life.

Pluto, as always, deserves special attention. Its pattern is interesting and requires more research because of the subtlety of its developmental nature and the brutality of its manifestation under certain conditions. For example, Pluto conjunct the Ascendant carries the potential for obsession. This potential may never manifest in its most positive or negative extreme unless subjected to special influences.

In one chart with out-of-bounds Pluto partile conjunction the Ascendant, the otherwise normal individual became obsessed with a female employee who subsequently married another man. From that moment the Pluto Ascendant employer made life miserable for the young couple by private threats, public embarrassment, physical threats and harassment. Although this individual was a successful businessman and perfectly normal in every other area of his life, the exhibition of his obsession was a clear threat to his economic standing and his reputation in the community. Despite this very real threat it proved impossible to persuade him to abandon his obsessional behavior, which eventually led to bankruptcy and legal restraint. Out-of-bounds Pluto has an unforgiving nature and its out-of-bounds cycle is reflected in its behavioral influence; once embarked on a bizarre course there will be no turning back from the inevitable destination.

Declination: Basic Information

What is declination? Declination is the parallel measure of the distance of the arc of the ecliptic from the equator as it inclines to and from the equator.

What is the ecliptic? The ecliptic marks the Sun's apparent route of travel by both longitude and declination as it appears to circle planet Earth.

What is celestial longitude? Celestial longitude is the measure of the zodiacal sign, degree and minute of the Sun's movement along the ecliptic and through the zodiac.

What is Earth's equator? The earth's equator is the circle that lies between the Earth's poles. When the earth's equator is extended into space it is also known as the equinoctial circle and/or the celestial equator.

How are longitude and declination related? These two measurements give us a constant position relationship between a specific sign, degree, and minute of longitude and it's corresponding degree and minute of declination along the ecliptic. Example: On March 21, 1993, the Sun at 0 Aries 53 is found at 0N23 declination. The Sun at 0 Aries 53 will *always* be found within a few minutes of 0N23 declination because the apparent orbit of the Sun around planet earth varies no more than a few minutes in its apparent orbit. We thus see that the Sun's position by longitude always gives the intersection of longitude and declination along the ecliptic and this *never* varies. This a rule to live by.

Is this important? It is important because we deal with planets and asteroids whose orbits are eccentric, i.e. their orbits do not coincide with the ecliptic and therefore a planet's longitude and declination may not relate to each other along the ecliptic. For example, on March 23, 1993, the Moon at 0 Aries 53, 4N47 was conjunct the Sun of March 21, 1993, by longitude but not by declination.

Note that the Sun at 4N47 must always be within a few minutes of 12 Aries 08 or 17 Virgo 52 and can *never* be found in both the longitudinal and declination position the Moon occupied on March 23, 1993.

The positions of the Moon, planets, and asteroids, like the Sun, are located by longitude *and* declination; but the Moon, planets and asteroids, being less stable and dependable in their orbits than the Sun, are not always found in the degree of declination associated with the longitudinal sign, degree, and minute occupied by the Sun when in that same sign, degree, and minute. When this happens (and it does happen frequently) these planets are located somewhere between the equator and the ecliptic (unless extreme declination places them outside the maximum ecliptic) and their influence must be traced to the ecliptic (where all activity takes place) by both longitude and declination in order to reveal their secrets.

An example horary chart demonstrates this point.

Attention is focused on three planets because although there seems to be no relationship between these three planets that can tie them together in any major exchange of energies, they proved to be the most important elements in the chart. The conversion of declination to longitude reveals conditions and activity that are not available through traditional longitudinal delineation.

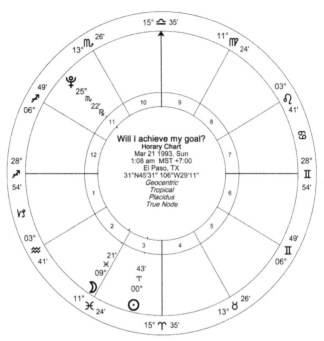

Horary question: I am about to undertake a new and important phase of professional and career activity. Will I encounter serious opposition, problems, personal attacks and/or treachery? Will I achieve my goal?

Sun: 0 Aries 43, 0N17

Moon: 9 Pisces 21, 3S27

Pluto: 25 Scorpio 23R, 4S48

Convert the declination of Pluto to longitude by finding the longitude of the Sun when in 4S48 declination.

Sun's declination at 4S48 intersects the ecliptic at 12 Libra 08 and 17 Pisces 52 and we will add these positions to our list because they represent Pluto's unknown activity and influence.

Now, to restate our position:

Sun: 0 Aries 43, 0N17 true given decl.

Moon: 9 Pisces 21, 3S43 given decl.

Pluto: 25 Scorpio 23R, 4S48 given decl.

Pluto: 4S48, given decl. = 12 Libra 08 on ecliptic

Pluto: 4S48 given decl. = 17 Pisces 52 on ecliptic

Part of Passionate Conviction: 12 Aries 52 = 5S05 decl. on ecliptic

The Part of Passionate Conviction has been added to the list because it is the only Arabian Part that relates so clearly to the above placements.

Transits of the Moon will show the development of significant aspects (relationships and/or events) between the three planets that can be revealed only through unlocking the secrets hidden by the anonymous face of declination. Observe:

March 21, 1993, GMT 24:17, transiting Moon at 17 Pisces 20 and 0S23 declination conjunction Pluto's declination point at 17 Pisces 52 and parallel the Sun's declination at 0N23.

March 22, 1993, GMT 16:33, transiting Moon at 25 Pisces 23 makes a straightforward longitudinal trine to Pluto at 25 Scorpio.

March 22, 1993, GMT 24:06, transiting Moon at 29 Pisces 07 opposition the Sun's solstice point at 29 Virgo 17.

March 23, 1993, GMT 2:38, transiting Moon at 0 Aries 23 conjunction the Sun while her declination at 4N35 makes the parallel opposition to Pluto at 4S48 and the parallel conjunction with the Part of Passionate Conviction at 5N09.

March 23, 1993, GMT 26:18, transiting Moon at 12 Aries 08 conjunction the Part of Passionate Conviction at 12 Aries 52, opposition Pluto's declination position at 12 Libra 07 and opposition Pluto's solstice point at 17 Pisces 53 with its own solstice point at 17 Virgo 53.

These aspects tell a clear story that begins when the Sun, an authority, takes a new and important course of action at the vernal equinox when it enters 0 Aries, the sign of its exaltation.

The Moon, always the agent of the Sun and busy on the Sun's business, is temporarily out of touch at 9 Pisces 21 3S27 but will soon become aware of Pluto's secret activity when it makes a longitudinal conjunction with Pluto's declination position at 17 Pisces 52, but cannot report to the Sun because its declination at 0S23 is contraparallel the Sun at 0N23. Nevertheless, the Moon moves to 25 Pisces 23 and makes a discrete, nonaggressive, diplomatic, direct contact with Pluto at 25 Scorpio 23 to confirm the Moon's deepest suspicions (Moon in suspicious Pisces trine Pluto).

When the Moon reaches 29 Pisces 07 to oppose the solstice point of the Sun a decision is taken, a turning point that will result in an agreement reached when the Moon is conjunct the Sun at 0 Aries 52 and presents his case against Pluto's activities with passionate conviction because the Moon's declination at 4N35 registers at 12 Aries to conjunct the Arabian Part of Passionate Conviction and oppose Pluto's secret activity at 12 Libra while opposing the solstice point of this activity at 17 Pisces 52.

The Moon, acting as the delegated authority for the Sun, moves to 12 Aries 08, where she acts on the Sun's mandate and her passionate conviction, exposes the unacceptable Plutonian behavior, delivers her ultimatum and surprise! surprise! guarantees that on April 1, 1993 the Sun will arrive at 12 Aries 08, 4N48 to enforce his ultimatum, opposing Pluto's nefarious behavior with passionate conviction, etc., repeating the aspects originally made by the Moon at 12 Aries 08 but *with authority*!

The client's sensitive, perceptive horary Moon, his personal radar, was, indeed, scanning for possible problems that he might encounter. Astrology confirmed his concern and intuition, helping him to deal with the problem of the unsuspected, hidden enemy working silently to prevent his success.

7. Is there any astrological rule to give this work authority? Yes. One of the cardinal rules of astrology states that *all activity takes place along the ecliptic*; therefore, every planet and asteroid

should be related to the ecliptic by both longitude and declination. As you work with this concept you will see that several new dimensions are added to the chart, hitherto unrevealed aspects as well as mobility, which allows for the movement of people represented by planets to be tracked in the chart. The rules for achieving this are:

A. The Sun is the only astrological body that is *always* true by longitude to its declination position on the ecliptic; therefore, it is the only totally reliable astrological body and longitude, and declination along the ecliptic must set the standard for all other celestial bodies.

B. The declination of all planets and asteroids must be coordinated with the longitudinal position of the Sun when the Sun is found in that degree and minute of declination occupied by the planet.

C. The longitudinal position of all planets and asteroids must be coordinated with the declination of the Sun when the Sun is found in that sign, degree and minute of longitude occupied by the planet.

8. Is there an easy way to find the coordinate of each degree and minute of declination with each sign, degree and minute of longitude along the ecliptic? Yes. See the Declination Longitude Conversion Table included in this book. This table is perfectly accurate but necessarily limited in its listings for the purpose of inclusion in this book.

It is also possible to turn to an ephemeris and find the degree of declination occupied by the Sun in any required sign and degree of longitude. You can then take the Sun's declination for the true declination on the ecliptic of a planet when in the same degree and minute of the Sun's longitude.

This process can be reversed by taking the given degree of a planet's declination and checking the ephemeris to determine what sign, degree, and longitude the Sun occupies on the ecliptic when in that degree of declination.

Pluto at 25 Scorpio 23 serves as an excellent example. By finding the Sun's declination for 25 Scorpio 23 you can identify yet another ecliptic action spot where Pluto's influence will be felt.

Example: Sun at 25 Scorpio 23 is intersected along the ecliptic at 19S08; therefore, Pluto at 25 Scorpio 23 will respond to a transiting or progressed third planet at 19S08 or 19N08 in parallel aspect to Pluto *regardless of the planet's sign and degree of longitude.*

It must be understood that working with declination is tedious at this point. Ideally, every computerized chart will someday produce a list of each occupied point of the chart and automatically provide declination-longitude conversion information.

The bar graphs presently used are helpful but they do not unlock the secrets hidden in declination. In the example just presented the Moon's only identifiable aspects to Pluto would have been the trine from 25 Pisces and finally the parallel when it arrived at 4N48. What can you do with that? Not much!

Longitude is the language of astrology and declination speaks volumes when translated into longitude along the ecliptic.

Latitude

A planet can achieve a modified out-of-bounds condition even though its declination is less than 23N/S28. This condition is easily recognized through the planet's latitude and its connection with longitude and declination.

Locate the position of the signs and degrees around earth's ecliptic, the longitude and the signs and degrees by which it is divided into twelve equal segments.

Declination measures the distance of the ecliptic by parallels to the equator for the purpose of recording the Sun's position by both longitude and declination as it moves through space.

Astronomers use six kinds of latitudinal measurement. One of these is celestial latitude, which is itself divided into three categories. One of these categories parallels the horizon and is irrelevant to this work. The second is, surprisingly, declination, with which we are quite familiar by now and which is measured by parallels to the equator, thus coordinating the degree of declination with each degree of longitude activated by the Sun as it moves through longitude and declination to set the ecliptic by two markers.

The third type of latitude is measured by parallels (both north and south) along the ecliptic and provides the information we seek in order to determine whether a planet at less than 23N/S28 declination may be outside the ecliptic, i.e., out of bounds.

To determine if you have a planet that is within the ecliptic limit of 23N/S28 declination but out of bounds by latitude the following rules should be applied:

- A planet in south declination less than 23S28 and south latitude greater than 0S30 is outside the ecliptic.

- A planet in south declination less than 23S28 and north latitude greater than 0N30 is within the ecliptic.

- A planet in north declination less than 23N28 and north latitude greater than 0N30 is outside the ecliptic.

- A planet in north declination less than 23N28 and south latitude greater than 0S30 is within the ecliptic.

- A planet in either north or south declination and either 0N30 or 0S30 is on the ecliptic where the action takes place.

Occasionally an asteroid does not conform readily to these rules. On January 15, 1983, the birthdate of Jenny, the abused child whose story is told in this book, Pallas at 24 Sagittarius 58, 4N13 declination, 27N34 latitude illustrates this point. However, once one's initial resistance to the idea of a body in a sign of south declination while in north declination and at such an

31

extreme degree of north latitude, it is possible to apply the rules and visualize this asteroid so far beyond the ecliptic that it describes an atom of life that was not only out of bounds but out of her element (Sagittarius of spiritual fire) and possibly not of this universe, a little spirit visiting this planet by some tragic error and only briefly.

Knowledge without understanding is useless. The time has come to describe the influence of planets that are out of bounds but not beyond the maximum ecliptic degree and therefore not beyond reasonable limits. Their key phrase is "more than should be expected within normal limitations and conditions."

These planets demonstrate normal conditions that are stretched to the limit at times as well as people who exhibit flexibility of opinion and adaptability that can be quite surprising at times.

Research indicates that the qualities of the fast-moving planets that fall into this category are up front, obvious, easily recognized and observed, in the clear.

Observations on Planets Outside the Ecliptic

In a general sense these planets identify people who in some fashion or other strive to achieve a high level performance within the rulership of the planet that has slipped outside the ecliptic. They often prove to be more adventurous, more daring than planets that are within the ecliptic by both declination and latitude. They allow themselves greater leeway.

Other factors in the chart must of course be taken into consideration. If an outside planet is badly afflicted they may simply give up all hope of ever being able to accomplish in that area and may become morose and unhappy if that outside planet is the chart ruler the result can be a feeling of aloofness, of not quite ever being a part of the group, of not quite fitting in. The individual might wonder why others do not recognize his or her excellence.

If the chart is strong and affords confidence in other areas the individual will probably overcome these negative attitudes and even come to laugh and accept them as merely another side of his or her unique nature.

The outside planets in many cases exercise a very subtle influence that is easily recognized only on close acquaintance, which is a very good reason why the astrologer should consider these planets carefully in delineating the chart. These subtle effects may eventually ruin a relationship if the partner does not understand their cause and effect. Experience indicates that where understanding does not exist, misunderstanding fills the void.

The heavy planets when outside the ecliptic have a different effect. Because of their slow and ponderous movement the influence they exercise constitutes a more concentrated focus on a life time interest and/or a lifelong condition or personal trait over which the native has little control.

The Turning Point

The Declination-Longitude Conversion Table is designed for easy conversion of planetary declination to the Sun's longitude on the ecliptic, as well as the reverse process. Both of these conversions are of serious importance in working with declination.

Although it is limited to a certain extent by the fact that the entries are computed for twenty-four hour intervals, it is accurate for the reported positions. While it may occasionally be necessary to extrapolate between two given positions, it will nevertheless prove accurate to considerably less than one degree of declination in most cases. It is remarkably simple to use.

To find a planet's longitude when in a particular degree of declination, simply search the first column for the planet's given declination and read across to find the longitudinal degree (north or south longitude) of the Sun when in that degree of declination. Once you have found the longitudinal position closest to the planet's given longitude you will also find the solstice point or co-declination position in the column beside that position.

Or, if you wish to convert longitude to its true declination on the ecliptic; search for that degree of longitude either north or south in the other four columns and refer across the page to the first column to find the Sun's declination when in the given degree of longitude.

Declination-Longitude Conversion Table

(Designed for easy conversion of planetary declination to the Sun's longitude on the ecliptic as well as the easy conversion of a planet's longitude to the Sun's declination on the ecliptic.)

Ecliptic Declination North/South	Ecliptic Longitude North	Ecliptic Longitude North	Ecliptic Longitude South	Ecliptic Longitude South
0N/S00 =	0 AR 00	30 VI 00	0 LI 00	30 PI 00
0N/S24 =	1 AR 00	29 VI 00	1 LI 00	29 PI 00
0N/S47 =	1 AR 59	28 VI 01	1 LI 59	28 PI 01
1N/S11 =	2 AR 59	27 VI 01	2 LI 59	27 PI 01
1N/S34 =	3 AR 58	26 VI 02	3 LI 58	26 PI 02
1N/S58 =	4 AR 58	25 VI 02	4 LI 58	25 PI 02
2N/S22 =	5 AR 57	24 VI 03	5 LI 57	24 PI 03
2N/S45 =	6 AR 57	23 VI 03	6 LI 57	23 PI 03
3N/S09 =	7 AR 56	22 VI 04	7 LI 56	22 PI 04
3N/S32 =	8 AR 55	21 VI 05	8 LI 55	21 PI 05
3N/S55 =	9 AR 54	20 VI 06	9 LI 54	20 PI 06
4N/Sl9 =	10 AR 54	19 VI 06	10 LI 54	19 PI 06
4N/S42 =	11 AR 53	18 VI 07	11 LI 53	18 PI 07
5N/S05 =	12 AR 52	17 VI 08	12 LI 52	17 PI 08
5N/S28 =	13 AR 51	16 VI 09	13 LI 51	16 PI 09
5N/S51 =	14 AR 51	15 VI 09	14 LI 51	15 PI 09
6N/S14 =	15 AR 50	14 VI 10	15 LI 50	14 PI 10
6N/S36 =	16 AR 49	13 VI 11	16 LI 49	13 PI 11
6N/S59 =	17 AR 48	12 VI 12	17 LI 48	12 PI 12
7N/S21 =	18 AR 47	11 VI 13	18 LI 47	11 PI 13
7N/S44 =	19 AR 46	10 VI l4	19 LI 46	10 PI 14
8N/S06 =	20 AR 45	9 VI 15	19 LI 45	9 PI 15
8N/S28 =	21AR 43	8 VI 17	21 LI 43	8 PI 17
8N/S50 =	22 AR 42	7 VI 18	22 LI 42	7 PI 18
9N/S12 =	23 AR 41	6 VI 19	23 LI 41	6 PI 19
9N/S33 =	24 AR 40	5 VI 20	24 LI 40	5 PI 20
9N/S55 =	25 AR 39	4 VI 21	25 LI 39	4 PI 21
10N/16 =	26 AR 37	3 VI 23	26 LI 37	3 PI 23
10N/S29 =	27 AR 36	2 VI 24	27 LI 36	2 PI 24
10N/S37 =	28 AR 34	1 VI 26	28 LI 34	1 PI 26
11N/S19 =	29 AR 33	0 VI 27	29 LI 33	0 PI 27

11N/S39 =	0 TA 32	29 LE 28	0 SC 32	29 AQ 28
12N/S00 =	1 TA 30	28 LE 30	1 SC 30	28 AQ 30
12N/S20 =	2 TA 29	27 LE 31	2 SC 29	27 AQ 31
12N/S40 =	3 TA 27	26 LE 33	3 SC 27	26 AQ 33
13N/S00 =	4 TA 25	25 LE 35	4 SC 25	25 AQ 35
13N/S19 =	5 TA 24	24 LE 36	5 SC 24	24 AQ 36
13N/S39 =	6 TA 22	23 LE 38	6 SC 22	23 AQ 38
13N/S58 =	7 TA 21	22 LE 39	7 SC 21	22 AQ 39
14N/S17 =	8 TA 19	21 LE 41	8 SC 19	21 AQ 41
14N/S35 =	9 TA 17	20 LE 43	9 SC 17	20 AQ 43
14N/S54 =	10 TA16	19 LE 44	10 SC 16	19 AQ 44
15N/S12 =	11 TA 14	18 LE 46	11 SC 14	18 AQ 46
15N/S30 =	12 TA 12	17 LE 48	12 SC 12	17 AQ 48
15N/S48 =	13 TA 10	16 LE 50	13 SC 10	16 AQ 50
16N/S05 =	14 TA 09	15 LE 51	14 SC 09	15 AQ 51

Declination-Longitude Conversion Table

Ecliptic Declination North/South	Ecliptic Longitude North	Ecliptic Longitude North	Ecliptic Longitude South	Ecliptic Longitude South
16N/S22 =	15 TA 07	14 LE 53	15 SC 07	14 AQ 53
16N/S39 =	16 TA 05	13 LE 55	16 SC 05	13 AQ 55
16N/S56 =	17 TA 03	12 LE 57	17 SC 03	12 AQ 57
17N/S12 =	18 TA 01	11 LE 59	18 SC 03	11 AQ 59
l 7N/S28 =	18 TA 59	11 LE 01	18 SC 59	11 AQ 01
17N/S44 =	19 TA 57	10 LE 03	19 SC 57	10 AQ 03
17N/S59 =	20 TA 55	9 LE 05	20 SC 55	9 AQ 05
l 8N/S15 =	21 TA 53	8 LE 07	21 SC S3	8 AQ 07
18N/S29 =	22 TA 51	7 LE 09	22 SC 51	7 AQ 09
18N/S44 =	23 TA 49	6 LE 11	23 SC 49	6 AQ 11
18N/S58 =	24 TA 46	5 LE 14	24 SC 46	5 AQ 14
19N/S11 =	25 TA 44	4 LE 16	25 SC 44	4 AQ 16
19N/S25 =	26 TA 42	3 LE 18	26 SC 42	3 AQ 18
19N/S38 =	27 TA 40	2 LE 20	27 SC 40	2 AQ 20
19N/S51 =	28 TA 37	1 LE 23	28 SC 37	1 AQ 23
20N/S04 =	29 TA 35	0 LE 25	29 SC 35	0 AQ 2S
20N/S16 =	0 GE 33	29 CA 27	0 SA 33	29 CP 27
20N/S28 =	1 GE 31	28 CA 29	1 SA 31	28 CP 29
20N/S39 =	2 GE 28	27 CA 32	2 SA 28	27 CP 32
20N/S50 =	3 GE 26	26 CA 34	3 SA 26	26 CP 34
21N/S21 =	4 GE 24	25 CA 36	4 SA 24	25 CP 36
21N/S12 =	5 GE 21	24 CA 39	5 SA 21	24 CP 39
21N/S22 =	6 GE 19	23 CA 41	6 SA 19	23 CP 41
21N/S31 =	7 GE 16	22 CA 44	7 SA l6	22 CP 44
21N/S41 =	8 GE 14	21 CA 46	8 SA 14	21 CP 46
21N/S50 =	9 GE 11	21 CA 49	9 SA 11	21 CP 49
21N/S58 =	10 GE 09	19 CA 51	10 SA 09	19 CP 51
22N/S06 =	11 GE 07	18 CA 53	11 SA 07	18 CP 53
22N/S14 =	12 GE 04	17 CA 56	12 SA 04	17 CP 56
22N/S22 =	13 GE 01	16 CA 59	13 SA 01	16 CP 59
22N/S29 =	13 GE 59	16 CA 01	13 SA 59	16 CP 01
22N/S35 =	14 GE 56	15 CA 04	14 SA 56	15 CP 04
22N/S41 =	15 GE 54	14 CA 06	13 SA 54	14 CP 06
22N/S47 =	l6 GE 51	13 CA 09	16 SA 51	13 CP 09
22N/S53 =	17GE 49	12 CA 11	17 SA 49	12 CP 11

22N/S58 =	18 GE 46	11 CA 14	18 SA 46	11 CP 14
23N/S02 =	19 GE 44	10 CA 16	19 SA 44	10 CP 16
23N/S07 =	20 GE 41	9 CA 19	20 SA 41	9 CP 19
23N/S10 =	21 GE 38	8 CA 22	21 SA 38	8 CP 22
23N/S14 =	22 GE 35	7 CA 25	22 SA 35	7 CP 25
23N/S17 =	23 GE 33	6 CA 27	23 SA 33	6 CP 27
23N/S19 =	24 GE30	5 CA 30	24 SA 30	5 CP 30
23N/S20 =	2S GE 27	4 CA 33	25 SA 27	4 CP 33
23N/S23 =	26 GE 24	3 CA 36	26 SA 24	3 CP 36
23N/S25 =	27 GE 22	2 CA 38	27 SA 22	2 CP 38
23N/S26 =	28 GE 19	1 CA 41	28 SA 19	1 CP 41
23N/S27 =	29 GE 17	0 CA 43	29 SA 17	0 CP 43

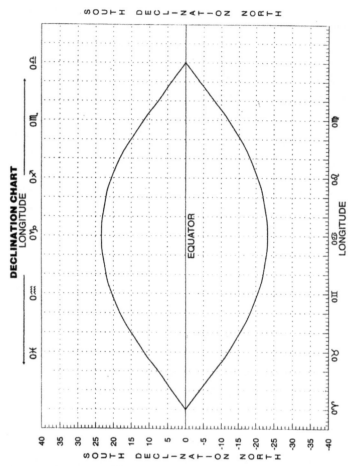

DECLINATION CHART
LONGITUDE

0♈   0♒   0♑   0♐   0♏   0♎

EQUATOR

0♓   0♌   0♋   0♊   0♉   0♈

LONGITUDE

40 35 30 25 20 15 10 5 0 -5 -10 -15 -20 -25 -30 -35 -40

SOUTH DECLINATION NORTH

The Declination Chart

The chart shown above is known as a declination chart. This chart was devised to help astrologers overcome the limitations of the round astrological chart and to enable us to place the positions of planets by both longitude and declination in order to visualize how declination reveals another dimension of potential and guidance.

The round chart is a one dimensional figure that does not

allow for the inclusion of any position or placement other than longitudinal. All planets appear to fall within the limited parameter of the circle representing the 360 degrees of longitude with no means of incorporating declination. Declination is just as legitimate a measure of a planet's position as longitude, it is simply unfortunate that there has never been a chart designed to allow us to place planets within the chart according to both their longitude and declination and their longitude and declination influence, which is referred to in this study as the declination/co-declination position.

This is probably a very good time to explain that when we speak of the declination/co-declination position we do not mean that the planet is actually in a degree of longitude other than that reported by computer or ephemeris. Declination/co-declination' identifies the degree of longitude indicated by the planet's declination on the ecliptic as a point of influence identified only by its given declination. The same is true when a planet is relocated on the ecliptic by the true declination of the longitudinal degree in which it is situated.

This then allows us six specific points of reference relating to each planet's influence. This sounds very confusing and complex but the trained astrological mind readily assimilates these added areas of influence after a little practice. It is in fact, not as complex as it sounds since the Jupiter, Saturn, Uranus, and Neptune will always be very close and very true by reported longitude to the reported declination. The Sun is always in the correct degree of declination for its given longitude. This is because the *Via Solis*, the Royal Highway of the Sun, is literally the ecliptic.

This leaves us only the Moon, Mercury, Venus, Mars, Pluto, and whatever asteroids are customarily applied to deal with on a multilevel plane. But even this isn't true all the time; only when these planets and asteroids are in eccentric orbits does the declination/co-declination position attain importance. Eccentric orbits are identified by declination positions that lead to a sign and

40

degree on the ecliptic that are a considerable distance from the given longitudinal position.

The Moon and Pluto when in their long-term out-of-bounds cycles, and the asteroids (little things whose orbits deserve a book of their own) are most frequently in eccentric orbits. Venus, Mercury and Mars are often quite close by longitude to their given declination position. The whole purpose of this exercise is that of determining which planets in any chart do not conform with the norm. Those planets need to be recognized and their areas of influence recorded for they mark the unusual, the unexpected, the unsuspected, the hidden influence that often confounds us as both astrologers and humans.

The final result, then, may not require much more effort than the simple longitudinal chart normally demands. The horary chart discussed in another chapter of this book is a good example of how this may simplify the process. Only three planets were necessary to give the answer. Those three planets were easily identified. First, the Sun at 0 Aries, a critical, urgent or important matter, the launching of a new program, process or plan, confirmed the validity of the question. Second, the Moon, always the radar of sensitivity and intuition, the search and identify planet, and finally, Pluto, whose declination/co-declination position reveals the extremity of its orbit and warns that something is not as it should be. In this case, the few minutes necessary to identify Pluto's hidden influence by its declination simplified the problem significantly. No other planets were used.

No other planets were necessary. How many hours have you spent chasing rulerships, and aspects, etc., etc., for hours around the chart, often finding that the tried and true rules didn't work in this particular instance?

Back to the declination chart. Imagine that you are standing far out in space on the plane of the equator and looking back to Earth, where you clearly see the shining path of the Sun, the ecliptic, as it moves through the longitudinal zodiac. Imagine also that you can see that path on the opposite side of Earth. From this position you will observe the ecliptic as an ellipse or oval that crosses Earth's equator at a 23 degree, 27 minute angle, the lost aspect, give or take a minute more or less.

If you look closely, you can see the measurement of the extent of the arc of the ecliptic by parallels of declination to the equator. Where the parallels of declination intersect the ecliptic they also intersect the longitudinal degree of the zodiac in which the Sun is always found when in that parallel of declination. And vice versa, the Sun's degree of longitude will always intersect the ecliptic in the same degree and minute of declination.

A planet can be located, and frequently is, in the vast space between the equator and the ecliptic; but when its declination (or parallel to the equator) is traced directly to the ecliptic it identifies the corresponding degree of longitude that it intersects on the ecliptic. This then is an area of important influence; the declination/co-declination influence of the planet. If that position is far from the planet's longitudinal position the same method should be applied in order to find the true declination influence where its longitude intersects declination on the ecliptic. This, too, will mark an important area of sensitivity. This is easily achieved through reference to the Declination-Longitude Conversion Table.

A thorough understanding of the declination chart will soon make its use unnecessary and you can rely on a simple listing of the declination/co-declination positions for quick and easy reference.

Child Abuse and Out-of-Bounds Planets

There are certain natural laws that drive human value systems on every level—mental, emotional, spiritual, physical, and financial. The most important of these natural laws may be that anything in over-abundance loses value. This is readily illustrated in the food industry, where an over-abundance of any particular food, whether wheat, oranges, or beef, drives the price (value) down. If the streets of this country had actually been paved in gold (as most of the world apparently believed in the late 1800s and early 1900s), it would never have been adopted as the U.S. monetary standard. This section addresses just such an over-abundance: the over-population of Earth and its effect on the treatment of children.

It is a curious fact that since the introduction of the birth control pill in the mid to late 1950s the entire world has experienced an explosion in population—not exactly what was intended by the developers and sponsors of the birth control pill who very accurately foresaw the dangers of over-population. The result in terms of child abuse is tragic, not curious, and the tragedy can be addressed only through each individual child's story. The result is, has always been, and always will be tragically predictable: the abuse of individual children because of an over-abundance of children and concomitant loss of their value. Substitute the word "life" for the words "child" and "children." The following is the story of a single child but it is also the story of millions of children at the end of the 20th century and the beginning of the 21st century.

Jenny

Jenny's chart shows the importance of working all aspects of declination related to longitude and longitude related to declination, the influence of prenatal eclipse points in natal charts, the effect of planets located on the ecliptic by both longitude and declination, and the influence of an out-of-bounds asteroid.

Prenatal Eclipse Points:

June 21, 1982, 29 Gemini 49, 23N49

July 6, 1982, 13 Capricorn, 22S30

July 20, 1982, 27 Cancer 47, 20N32

December 15, 1982, 23 Sagittarius 16, 23S15

December 30, 1982, 8 Cancer 29, 23N10

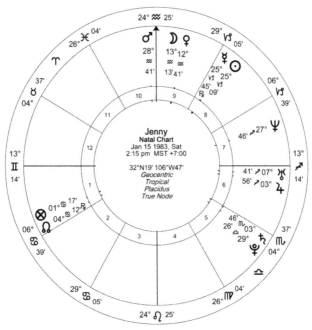

Out-of-Bounds Asteroid:
Ceres, the mother, the maternal instinct
14 Capricorn 45, 25S26
See table for true declination; 14 Capricorn 45 = 22S35

To bring 25S26 to the ecliptic:
> Ceres 25S26 declination
> minus <u>23S28</u> ecliptic max
> minus <u>1:58</u> from ecliptic

Ceres 21S30 co-declination
Out-of-bounds Ceres:
21S30 = 22 Capricorn 44
> 7 Sagittarius 16

Note: Neither rectification nor delineation of a natal chart should be undertaken without listing every prenatal eclipse that has occurred during the gestation period. It is not necessary to differentiate between lunar and solar eclipses in this instance.

Given longitude of planets corrected for true declination on the ecliptic (see table):

Moon, 13 Aquarius 12 = 16S40

Mercury, 25 Capricorn 46, 21S21

Venus, 12 Aquarius 43 = 17S00

Mars, 28 Aquarius 42 = 11S50

Jupiter, 3 Sagittarius = 21S00

Saturn, 3 Scorpio 47 = 12S50

Uranus, 7 Sagittarius 42 = 22S25

Neptune, 27 Sagittariius 48 = 23S25

Pluto, 29 Libra 27 = 11S19

Ceres, 14 Capricorn = 22S35

Pallas, 24 Sagittarius 58 = 23S18

Given declination of planets corrected for true longitude on the ecliptic (see table):

Moon, 20S02 = 29 Scorpio 0 Aquarius

Mercury, 18S00 = 21 Scorpio, 9 Aquarius

Venus, 18S27 = 22 Scorpio 51, 7 Aquarius 09

Mars, 12S54 = 4 Scorpio 25, 25 Aquarius 35

Jupiter, 20S07 = 0 Sagittarius, 29 Capricorn

Saturn, 10S28 = 27 Libra 30, 2 Pisces 30

Uranus, 21S28 = 7 Sagittarius 16, 22 Capricorn 44

Neptune, 22S13 = 12 Sagittarius 04, 17 Capricorn 56

Pluto, 4N38 = 12 Aries 00, 18 Virgo 00

Ceres, 25S26 corrected to the ecliptic =

Ceres, 21S30 = 22 Capricorn 44, 7 Sagittarius 16

Pallas: 4N13 = 19 Virgo 11 Aries

The listings given above provide planetary aspects and areas of influence that are not identifiable until the given positions that normally accompany every chart undergo the conversion process giving the complex influence of each planet.

The location of Pallas, the asteroid representing the daughter, in Jenny's chart is quite radical and for this reason deserves special attention.

Pallas at 24 Sagittarius 58 (a sign of south declination) is reported in declination 4N13 (a celestial body in a sign of south declination with its declination position falling in signs of north longitude?) with an unheard of and extreme latitude at 27N34 warns of unusual conditions or circumstances and requiring special attention. As usual it is necessary to locate the true declination of its given longitude on the ecliptic by referring to the Table of Equivalent Longitude-Declination where we find that 24 Sagittarius 58 intersects the ecliptic at 23S18 aspecting by both longitude and declination the prenatal eclipse of December 15, 1982. This is the only true parallel conjunction (conjunction by longitude and parallel by declination) that Pallas makes, although by declination she makes simple parallel aspects to the prenatal eclipses of December 30, 1982, July 6, 1982, and June 29, 1982. Bearing in mind that all eclipses represent electromagnetically disturbed areas in the chart, this baby was doomed to an extremely turbulent life. You will have noticed that the unusual declination of this asteroid gives an equivalent longitude of 10 Aries 50 and 19 Virgo 10. These peculiarities seem to indicate that she was never destined for this planet.

Viewed in the traditional fashion, Jenny's chart does not exhibit afflictions of such severity as to cause extreme alarm. In fact, natal Venus of love partile conjunction the mother Moon in partile trine to the Ascendant seems to give a strong measure of protection. The partile conjunction of the father Sun and Jenny's personal ruler Mercury on the solstice point of benefic Jupiter reinforces the idea that this is a beloved child. Even Uranus, ruler

46

of the mother tenth house would appear to be moderated in its eccentricity by conjunction with jovial, friendly Jupiter. The Part of Fortune and the North Node (Jupiterian in effect) rising also seem to indicate good fortune. Mars, a malefic planet, in close conjunction to the Midheaven and trine Pluto, offers the greatest threat, but the traditional benefic aspects that we have observed would seem to lessen the threat even though it is trine Pluto, which is in an out-of-sign conjunction with Saturn. Using traditional methods this is not an extremely afflicted chart.

Even the parallels of declination as traditionally applied support this opinion. The Moon at 20S02 is parallel Jupiter, Venus at 18S27 is parallel Mercury, Jenny's personal ruler. Mars, Saturn, and Pluto make no parallels. Uranus parallels the Sun and Neptune but produces no major threat to the child's welfare. Please note that all of these parallels are harmonious, i.e., all in south declination, according to traditional delineation.

As previously indicated, the unusual condition of Pallas by longitude, declination, and latitude is a red alert to the astrologer. Ceres out of bounds is a second alert and the extreme number of prenatal eclipse points during the gestation period constitutes the third alert. All of these are important warnings identifiable only through the unorthodox methods presented here.

Because the given longitude and declination of the planets give little or no information about the cause of Jenny's trauma, it is necessary to look at the aspects made by the true declination of each planet's natal longitude to the given natal declination of the planets.

Moon: 13 Aquarius 12 = 16S40, and Venus, 12 Aquarius 43 = 17S00: parallel conjunction but making no aspects by longitude or declination to other planets.

Mars: 28 Aquarius 42 = 11S50 and makes no parallel aspect to Jenny's personal ruler.

Mercury: 25 Capricorn 46 retrograde = 21S21 and makes a

parallel to co-declination out-of-bounds Ceres (the mother) at 21S30, a parallel to Uranus (ruler of the maternal tenth house) at 21S28, a parallel to the prenatal eclipse at 20N32. The retrograde condition describes a child who is irrevocably tied (by parallel) to a mother who is out of touch with reality (Ceres out of bounds) deranged and disturbed (because parallel to Uranus and the disturbing prenatal eclipse).

Jupiter: ruler of the separation seventh cusp, co-ruler of the end of family affairs eleventh cusp, associated with courts of law, at 3 Sagittarius 57 = 21S00 and makes a parallel to the father Sun, ruler of the end of affairs fourth cusp, a parallel to out-of-bounds Ceres, and a parallel to Uranus, ruler of the maternal tenth cusp. The court associated with child protective services favored returning Jenny to her family more than once, to Jenny's great cost.

Saturn: ruler of the eighth house of death, co-ruler of the maternal tenth, conjunction the physical sixth cusp at 3 Scorpio 47 (12S50) is parallel Mars (natally found at 12S54), the traditional physical cruelty aspect.

Uranus: 7 Sagittarius 42 = 22S25 parallel Neptune, ruler of drugs and addiction at 23S25, Ceres at 14 Capricorn 45 = 22S35, and Pallas (the daughter) 24 Sagittarius 58 = 22S35 are all involved in parallel aspects to four of the prenatal eclipse points at 23N10, 23S15, 22S30 and 23N28. The mother and her child share the disturbed world of the mother's madness and the child's reality. This must be the real definition of Hell on earth.

Pluto: 29 Libra 27 = 11S19 parallel Saturn, 3 Scorpio 47 = 10S28 to describe the outcome, death by violence and murder— a brutal death.

First Impressions

For about five years I had the opportunity to work with child protective services in a state that must remain, for obvious reasons, anonymous due to the *ex officio* nature of the enquiries. Several lawyers and social workers who sometimes served as foster parents prior to child protective services judicial hearings to decide the disposition of these abused children, consulted me regarding the fate of these children. They found it very disturbing that these children were invariably returned to the abusive parents as long as those parents gave minimal lip service to rehabilitation. The results, of course, of these rulings were all too predictable. Without exception these concerned people wished to know if there was anything that could be done to provide these children a good life. Unfortunately, the little girl whose chart is examined here was not allowed any saving graces in her chart and she lived less than two and one half years.

She first came to the attention of child protective services when she was about nine months old, her parents having brought her to the hospital in serious condition, saying that she had been injured in a fall. Her injuries were typical of child abuse and were routinely reported by the hospital and medical personnel who treated her. Those injuries included old and new burns (as in cigarette burns), old and new bruises on the body and extremities, and serious head injuries. So serious in fact that she was permanently brain damaged. At this point she was placed with a social worker-foster parent who kept her for several months while child protective services investigated the parents and enrolled them in rehabilitation.

At the time of her birth the parents were 17 and 18 years of age and had another child, a boy, about 2 or 3 years older than the little girl. He also showed signs of child abuse, although not so severe as his sister's. Both parents were drug addicted and unemployed with no visible means of support.

After about six months the court saw fit to return the little girl to her parents and she remained with them for a few months until it became obvious that she was being abused again. For the second time the girl was placed with the social worker-foster mother for a few months and then returned to the parents.

On April 21, 1985, the parents again brought her to the hospital, claiming that she had fallen again or had an accident (they were unclear about this). The difference was that this time she was dead.

Her autopsy revealed fresh burns, bruises, internal injuries and massive brain injuries associated with having been shaken so hard that the retinas of her eyes had been torn loose and her brain severely damaged by the shaking, literally having been bounced around in the confines of her little skull.

This time child protective services placed the mother, who was pregnant again, in institutional rehabilitation.

Because this tragic case is typical of these cases, it was chosen as an example of the interaction between the charts of the parents and the child.

Jenny's chart was studied in the preceding chapter. Now it will be interesting to look at the mother's chart in order to understand why she was capable of treating this child so cruelly. The father was not the major problem in this case. In fact, Jenny was returned to her parents on the strength of the known fact that the father sometimes controlled his wife and protected his daughter. He was simply irresponsible and child protective services felt it was possible to help him to adjust to a more constantly responsible attitude.

No data was available for the parents except their birth dates. For this reason a new form of relationship chart between the child and each parent, which has proven invaluable in many other instances, is included in this study. You will also note that n these charts every prenatal eclipse that occurred during the nine-month gestation period prior to the birth of the mother has been listed. Additionally, all planets, including out-of-bounds planets, have been submitted to declination/co-declination techniques in order to identify important correlations hidden by declination.

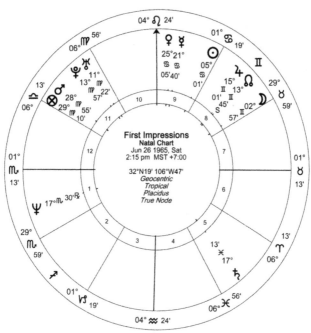

First impression charts illustrate the child's perception of the parents at the moment of birth, marking the first parental impression upon the child as well as the parents' first perception and impression of the child. These charts might well be called "imprint" charts. They are very helpful in delineating child-parent relationships and why each sibling in a family usually has his or her own impression of the parents and a very different relationship with the parents than that of other of his or her siblings.

Declination:

Ceres, 0 Aries 04, 10S27

Moon, 19N47

O-O-B Mercury, 23N36; corrected to 21N45

Venus, 22N31

Mars, 0N48

Jupiter, 22N04

Saturn, 5S50
Uranus, 8N00
Neptune, 15S20
Pluto: 19N20
Arabian Parts
Death, 28 Libra 16
Violence, 5 Cancer 15
Murder, 5 Pisces 42
Prenatal Eclipses:
8 Gemini 43
22 Sagittarius 50

Jenny's chart was calculated according to the data given. However, in calculating the chart for the mother, because of the lack of information, tradition has been abandoned and the chart was calculated combining the mother's birth date with the birth time and place given for the child's birth (mother's birth date, June 26, 1965). Further than that the mother's chart was treated in every particular as if all data were correct. This means that appropriate Arabian Parts were computed, prenatal eclipse points for the mother's gestation period were included and the Moon's longitudinal and declination positions were accepted as correct.

The traditional methods of chart comparison, when applied to Jenny's natal chart and the mother's first impression chart, provide some interesting first impressions. With Jennie's natal Saturn conjunct the mother's Ascendant it is certainly reasonable to assume that the mother considers Jennie an unwanted burden and responsibility. More important, the mother's Ascendant conjunction Jenny's Saturn inspires fear and possibly loathing of the mother. The mother's Moon at 2 Gemini 57 is conjunct the solstice point of Jenny's prenatal eclipse at 27 Cancer 47 to activate constant emotional disturbances in the relationship. The mother's natal Mars at 28 Virgo 56 in a partile quincunx to Jenny's natal Mars at 28 Aquarius 42 is yet another markedly upsetting aspect, and finally the mother's natal Ceres, the maternal principle, at 10S27 is partile parallel conjunction Jenny's natal Saturn at 10S28. Powerful indications of rejection, anger, and resentment are expressed here and compounded by the mother's Part of Death at 28 Libra 16 partile conjunction Jenny's natal Pluto while the mother's Point of Death (Mars-Saturn) at 23 Sagittarius 05 is partile conjunction Jenny's prenatal eclipse as well as her own at 23 Sagittarius 16.

The mother's natal South Node conjunction Jenny's natal Ascendant is an unrelenting karmic tie, and although the mother's natal Jupiter at 15 Gemini 02 seemingly should allow some benefit or mitigating circumstances, even mighty Jupiter seems unable to overcome the terrible conflict in this relationship. There are other traditional indications of the relationship conflict between mother and daughter but none so severe as those exhibited when the longitude of the mother's natal planets is located by declination on the ecliptic where we see very clearly the mother's total rejection of this child.

But before looking at those aspects we should note that the mother was born with natal Mercury out of bounds, which in all likelihood contributed to mental and neurological instability. In addition, the mother's natal Ceres, the mother asteroid, the maternal principle, is conjunct the solstice point of her natal Mars, leading to speculation that she herself may have been an unwanted child with an angry mother as well as the angry mother of an unwanted child.

When the mother's natal planets are relocated to the true ecliptic declination that corresponds with their longitudinal positions we see a very clear picture of her rejection, alienation, opposition, and separation from Jenny.

Mother's planets located on ecliptic according to the true declination of their longitude	Jenny's natal planets found in declination within one degree of the mother's true planetary declination
Moon, 20N50, par. opp.	Moon, Jupiter, Uranus, Sun, Ceres
Mercury, 21N45, par. opp.	Sun, Uranus, Neptune
Venus, 21N20, par. opp.	Sun, Uranus
Jupiter, 22N38, par. opp.	Neptune
Saturn, 5S00, par. opp.	Pluto
Neptune, 17S04, par. opp.	Mercury

In addition, many of the mother's planets make parallel aspects to the declination positions of Jenny's sensitive prenatal eclipse points.

It would be very difficult to find stronger indications of total rejection than these; a veritable nightmare for a helpless infant and no escape but death.

Murder Out-of-Bounds

This section explores the devastating effect of rejection and alienation associated with the out-of-bounds Moon and the prenatal epoch chart in order to see how effectively it supports the declination of the natal chart.

Charts come in as many varieties as the people and lives they describe. Most lives incorporate the same events: illnesses, accidents, marriages, deaths. But no two lives are identical just as no two charts are identical.

Jenny's chart, previously discussed, is the chart of a severely abused child. Larry's chart, which is included here, is also the chart of an abused child. These two charts, although describing the same root problem, are vastly different. Jenny suffered abuse of an extreme physical nature and shorter duration than that of Larry, whose misery was largely emotional and lasted much longer. Jenny died at the hands of her parents; Larry's adoptive parents died at the hands of Larry. Jenny's chart on the surface is really too good to be true when compared to the facts of her life; the real circumstances are exposed only through careful examination of relationships between natal longitudinal planets and their declination and co-declination positions. Larry's chart is basically quite straightforward once the out-of-bounds Moon and her influence is recognized. There is really no need to examine the declination and co-declination of all the other planets, although such a study would provide added information.

It should be noted that when the natal Moon is out of bounds it is wise to set the prenatal epoch chart. If the natal Moon and the prenatal epoch Moon are the only out-of-bounds planets, you can be sure that the chart you are working with is a critical chart and the position and condition of both the natal out-of-bounds Moon and the prenatal out-of-bounds Moon and her declination and co-declination positions in both these charts will provide a mass of revealing information.

The charts and story that follow are an amazing demonstration of the ability of astrology to reveal the human heart and soul and spirit; the conscious, unconscious, and subconscious mind and the effect of the pressure of a stressful life on a young human being.

Larry, born with the Moon out of bounds, was rejected for one reason or another by seven sets of parents before his seventh birthday. His case history makes it clear that these rejections were because of the immaturity and/or instability of the adults involved. He was a beautiful baby and child who wanted to be loved and to belong to someone. As time passed and he was abused one way and another by various of his would-be parents, he developed emotional insecurities that did nothing to improve his situation or adaptability. Finally, the eighth attempt was at least legally successful and he was adopted in July 1974 by a couple with whom he had lived since June 16, 1973, who subsequently adopted two more children: another boy, Michael, and a girl about eight years younger than the two boys who were born less than a year apart. Larry killed his adoptive parents on the evening of January 16, 1984. The intervening years between adoption and murder were very painful ones.

Larry's first year with his adoptive parents, Bob and Kay, was the most idyllic period of his life; his parents responded to his needs to a much greater extent than he had ever experienced before and he, in response, overcame the nocturnal incontinence that had plagued his life and the life of foster parents, as well as an inordinate appetite that led him, as early as age three or four, on midnight forays to the kitchen where he ate everything he could et his hands on.

No more than three or four months after Larry's formal adoption, Michael, just six months older than Larry, was adopted, and although Larry had been with the family longer, Michael became the older son in the scheme of family relationships and Larry began to see a different side of his parents.

Larry and Michael bonded very well but as time progressed and Bob and Kay began to exhibit a severe, critical, and punitive attitude toward Michael. Larry became ever more fearful that he would be treated the same way and so, for the next five or six years, his emotional insecurity and fear began to increase in direct proportion to the increasing degree of parental pressure, extreme disciplinary techniques, and criticism applied to his brother Michael. While Michael bore the brunt of parental abuse and could at least try to defend himself directly, Larry did not dare to openly defend his brother while at the same time living in fear of what would happen to him if his parents disowned Michael. Would he than become the scapegoat? Rejected again?

In 1978, Bob and Kay adopted a three-yea-old girl. Both boys were delighted to have a sister and loved her dearly and her welfare became a vital issue for them, particularly for Larry, who began to worry about her future after he and Larry grew up and moved out of the family home. Would she then become the victim? The thought was intolerable to him and the temperature in Larry's pressure cooker increased.

It is worth noting that both Larry and Michael were judged to be learning disabled, which displeased their parents markedly. The parents used punitive methods in order to try to force the boys to do better. As usual, Michael was the principal focus of their punishment. Larry reacted to Michael's punishment with both resentment and increased insecurity; the threat of punishment is often worse than the punishment itself, due to its psychological effect.

Bob, the father, was described as an iron fisted and rigidly intolerant man with a high temper. Kay was described as more pliant but emotionally unstable with a tendency to take extreme views of normal and harmless matters; she took second place to her husband in the area of family authority. Both parents were extremely religious, some thought radical in their religious devotion, and apparently related very strongly to the "spare the rod and spoil the child" point of view.

In January 1980, Larry's fears became reality. Michael was literally thrown out of the family home, and the parents petitioned the state to relieve them of their responsibility. State records show that state case workers asked the juvenile court to declare him a child in need of assistance because his parents were either unable or unwilling to give him proper care and attention. Throughout Michael's case history he is described as trying very hard to please his parents while at the same time trying to defend himself against their abuse. Even after expulsion from the family he continued to nourish the hope that the people he loved would let him come home; he reinforced this with letters and phone calls to his parents, who refused to respond. Only Larry remained in touch and in sympathy with Michael.

From the time of Michael's expulsion from the family Larry's secret nightmare began to come true. Both parents began to focus their critical attention on him. He became the principal victim, the scapegoat that his parents appeared to require. His concern for the welfare of his little sister increased and he had less ability to defend himself than his brother Michael had demonstrated. He was at the most vulnerable psychological and emotional period of life, an adolescent, not quite fourteen. The next three years would witness the manifestation of his mental, emotional, and physical abuse (made doubly painful by the loss of his favored son status) that Larry had feared for years. Late at night on January 16, 1984, the pressure cooker exploded.

Larry was born August 25, 1966, with natal Moon out of bounds at 26S30, which is brought to its true declination and longitude on the ecliptic by means of the simple mathematical formula:

1. Subtract the maximum ecliptic declination from the given declination of the planet.

2. Subtract the difference of the product of Step 1 from the maximum declination of the ecliptic. The result of Step 2 gives the position by both declination and longitude of the planet's influence on the ecliptic where all events take place. Example:

	26S30 declination of natal Moon
minus	<u>23S28</u> maximum declination of the ecliptic
minus	3:02 difference
from	<u>23S28</u> maximum declination of the ecliptic
	20S26 declination of the out-of-bounds Moon's influence on the ecliptic.

Refer to the Declination-Longitude Conversion Table, where 20S26 declination is found to correlate with longitudinal positions at 28 Capricorn 28 and 1 Sagittarius 32. These placements should be identified as out of bounds and inserted in the natal chart.

The natal out-of-bounds Moon renders the child super-sensitive emotionally, unstable of temperament and disposition, driven by a desire for acceptance and approval. A cautionary word:

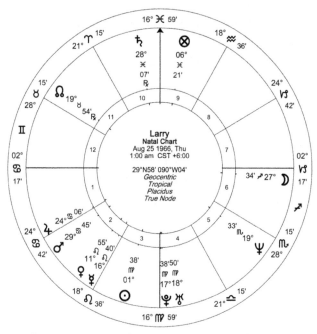

these influences can vary from major to minor by position, aspect, etc., and, in some cases, can be completely overcome by positive influences. Larry's chart was chosen for this study because it provided no mitigating circumstances that could work to minimize his difficulties. It is an extreme example of the cruelty of life under an out-of-bounds Moon.

Larry's chart exhibits many red flags that direct the attention to conditions of marked importance in his life. The out-of-bounds Moon's pervasive influence is reflected in all the prospective mothers who came and went in his life, as well as in his own nature. He is sensitive, insecure, unstable, family oriented, and inclined to extremes of emotional feeling and behavior. Most males born with the Moon out-of-bounds love their mothers, try desperately to gain their love and approval, and are painfully sensitive to their disapproval. This condition often continues long after mother is dead and gone. It is a tragedy that they often achieve many goals but rarely, if ever, win the acceptance and approval of the mother. Larry had these placements:

O-O-B Moon, 26S30

    corrected to 20S26 = 28 Capricorn 28, 1 Sagittarius 32

Prenatal Eclipse

    28 Taurus 57

Arabian Parts

    Part of Death, 29 Cancer 27

    Point of Death, 28 Taurus 57

    Part of Murder, 2 Cancer 18

When working with charts containing out-of-bounds planets, particularly the out-of-bounds Moon, let that planet lead you into the most critical aspects of life. Larry's chart is a classic example of this technique.

The out-of-bounds natal Moon at 27 Sagittarius 34 is involved in a painful square to Saturn in the tenth house (a fall from favor) and opposes the solstice point (turning point) of the Ascendant to create uncertainty and insecurity through his inability to foresee either the effect of his own behavior or that of others. The natal out-of-bounds Moon also makes a yod (a fateful aspect; a worthy effort for an unworthy cause) to the prenatal eclipse at 29 Taurus (something to weep about) and violent Mars conjunct the Part of Death. This is severely emphasized by the out-of-bounds declination and co-declination Moon at 28 Capricorn 28 in opposition to natal Mars and the Part of Death at 29 Cancer (both at the end of the rope, getting ready to act; forced to act) with Mars in its fall in the maternal and familial sign of Cancer (violence in the family) in the second house of the immediate future (that which is sure to happen before too long). From this point it is only a matter of time.

Please note that the prenatal eclipse at 28 Taurus 57 (the weeping degree). All natal charts should list all eclipses that occur between conception and birth. Prenatal eclipse points identify electromagnetically disturbed areas of considerable intensity and aspects to those points are related to some of the most disturbing events in life.

Before turning our attention to Larry's prenatal epoch chart, it is truly shocking to see that the Part of Peril and the Part of Murder are both partile conjunction the Ascendant at birth, while the Part of Murder and Violence at 20 Scorpio 52 is partile conjunction Neptune, ruler of the secret and innermost emotions and co-ruler of the mother tenth cusp, and the punishing South Node at 19 Scorpio 34 and 55. The violent and cruel Mars/Saturn midpoint is conjunct the prenatal eclipse at 28 Taurus 57. The message of this chart is incredibly explicit, simple to read, inevitable and totally unacceptable to the twentieth century mentality, which rejects the possibility that free will does not reign supreme.

When Larry's chart is progressed for the various events of his unfortunate life the pattern is fulfilled in all particulars: the disorder of his early years, his adoption, the adoption of his brother and sister, and the murder of his parents.

Prenatal Epoch Charts and Out-of-Bounds Planets

The prenatal epoch chart, also known as the conception chart, is an invaluable aid to astrologers but not often used because the astrologer frequently encounters problems in finding the correct prenatal epoch or conception chart.

The rules for finding the prenatal epoch chart basically accurate but must not be considered infallible. Some degree of flexibility is required. Larry's chart is an excellent example of the exception to the rule.

1. Larry's natal Moon is increasing in light and below the Ascendant, indicating that conception occurred *more than* ten lunar months prior to the birth date. Larry's case history states that he was more than a month premature.

When the Moon is increasing in light at birth it will be found in the sign that is rising in the natal chart. Larry's Ascendant at birth is 2 Cancer 18.

2. If the Moon is increasing at birth, its place will be rising at the time of conception on the day of conception. Larry's chart would then require that the prenatal epoch chart Ascendant be found at 27 Sagittarius 34. The rule is not reliable in this case because a deviation from normal is proven in the discrepancy between the known length of time of gestation period and the rule that is supposed to establish the length of the gestation period.

3. The third rule requires that the Moon must be in the exact degree of the Ascendant of the natal chart. A more accurate rule dictates that the Moon must, in fact, be allowed a couple of degrees leeway on either side of the natal Ascendant.

4. The Ascendant of the prenatal epoch chart *must* occupy the exact degree and minute of the natal Moon's natal position or its opposition position.

5. The rules place marked emphasis on the measurement of the lunar month. This is completely wrong because the lunar month equals 29 days 12 hours 43 minutes 11.5 seconds and marks the Moon's return to its original position *in relation* to the Sun. The correct monthly measure is the sidereal month, which equals 27.322 days or 27 days 7 hours 43 minutes 11.5 seconds and marks the Moon's return to its exact natal chart longitudinal position 27 days before or after the event.

The prenatal epoch chart will be the basis for the progression to the year in which Larry murdered his parents, for the specific purpose of demonstrating how accurately the subject's epoch chart reflects the events and the timing of events that occurred in his life. This conception chart should never be used to the exclusion of the natal chart; its usefulness should be utilized in verifying and sometimes enhancing the reading of the natal chart.

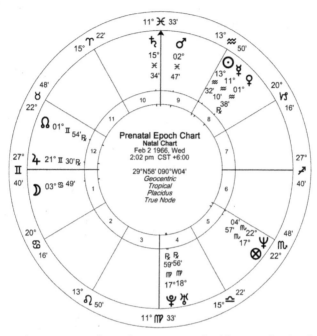

Prenatal Epoch Chart
Natal Chart
Feb 2 1966, Wed
2:02 pm CST +6:00

29°N58' 090°W04'
Geocentric
Tropical
Placidus
True Node

In the practice of astrology it is invaluable as a check of the accuracy of the natal chart and especially important if the astrologer has rectified the natal chart from an unknown birth time. If the rectified natal chart is accurate, the prenatal chart will progress satisfactorily for the events used in the rectification, which is extremely reassuring for a practicing astrologer.

The prenatal epoch chart functions like any natal chart, i.e., by progressions and directions to the prenatal positions; but it also progresses and directs to the positions in the natal chart. In fact, the natal chart and the prenatal chart interact throughout life to provide a greater depth of understanding and revealing information.

Larry murdered his parents the night of January 16, 1984. The time was never precisely established, although it was generally accepted that it occurred around 10:00 or 11:00 p.m. Larry called the police at 7:13 a.m., January 17, 1984. The transiting Moon at the time of the murders and the time of the call was out of bounds; in fact, throughout his life the out-of-bounds Moon plagued Larry's every move.

The transiting out-of-bounds Moon's declination and co-declination positions are found at 3 Gemini 26 and 26 Cancer 34, just two days before the murders. These out-of-bounds Moon positions conjunction the natal declination positions of Mars (21N09 = 3 Gemini 35 and 26 Cancer 25), square prenatal eclipse Mars at 2 Pisces 48, which in turn is trine the natal Ascendant and the prenatal eclipse Moon's given position at 3 Cancer 49: the ultimate in self-destructiveness describing both Larry and his mother. Shortly before the murders Larry had fallen in love for the first time. Unfortunately, when his mother discovered this she was extremely critical and derisive of his girlfriend and his relationship with her. When transiting Moon, in its eccentric cycle, formed a conjunction with the prenatal eclipse out-of-bounds Moon and natal declination and co-declination Mars at 3 Gemini 30, thus triggering this very damaging complex of aspects on January 14, 1984; out-of-bounds, both mother and child went too far. Both action and reaction were extreme.

By Larry's birth date in 1983, his progressed and directed Midheavens had moved to form a conjunction with natal Saturn at 28 Pisces 07, ruler of the eighth house of death in the natal and prenatal eclipse charts. The directed Ascendant moved to 14 Cancer 46 and the progressed Ascendant moved to 12 Cancer 18 to bracket the prenatal eclipse Part of Death at 13 Capricorn 56 by opposition. The directed Moon at 21 Cancer 00 was trine the prenatal eclipse Part of Murder at 20 Scorpio 12, the natal South Node (19 Scorpio 55), and natal Neptune (19 Scorpio 34). Progressed Ceres at 12 Aries 09 was conjunct the solstice point of prenatal eclipse Pluto (17 Virgo 59) and prenatal eclipse Uranus (18 Virgo 51), a truly frightening conjunction. There is a great deal of action within the chart but the transiting out-of-bounds Moon at 3 to 4 Gemini triggered the event in conjunction with the declination-codeclination natal Mars at 3 Gemini 35 and the out-of-bounds prental eclipse Moon's declination-codeclination position at 3 Gemini 26.

Ecliptic Action

When working with declination it is necessary to establish and understand the relationship between declination, longitude, and the ecliptic, each of which is a means of measuring and locating bodies and important astrological positions in space. In a manner of speaking one might say that declination and longitude are the road signs of the royal highway of the Sun, the ecliptic.

Declination is a series of measurements that are parallel to and north or south of the celestial equator or the plane of Earth's equator extended into space.

The ecliptic, also known as the *Via Solis*, is the path of the Sun's apparent orbit around Earth. It is along this orbit that the 360 degrees of the zodiac are measured by longitude and the orbit itself is inclined at an angle of 23N/S28 degrees of declination from the equator. Because of the obliquity of the angle of the orbit as it inclines from the equator, the signs and degrees of longitude do not advance at a perfectly even pace along the degrees of declination on the ecliptic. If the ecliptic were laid out along the plane of the equator our days and nights would be perfectly equal at all times and the Sun's movement would be seen to be a perfectly even progression in time, longitude and declination.

Our Universe is the perfect perpetual motion machine and the Sun through the nature of its composition and the energy created by its orbit, electromagnetically fuses and energizes the degree and minute of declination and its matching degree and minute of longitude along the Sun's path as they are simultaneously occupied by the Sun. The ecliptic is an elliptical figure (i.e., in its relation to Earth's equator and the celestial equator);

cutting diagonally across the equator and through space where every degree and minute of longitude that the Sun transits along the ecliptic is related to the degree and minute of declination that coincides with that specific degree and minute of longitude along the ecliptic.

These corresponding degrees are energized as the Sun moves along the ecliptic year after year. The most serious generation of energy occurs at longitude 0 Aries and 0 Libra and their related declination degrees 0N00 and 0S00. Another serious generation of energy is felt at 0 Cancer and 0 Capricorn (the peak of the solar arc's declination) and their related declination degrees at 23N28 and 23828, the points of near inertia where the Sun's movement in declination slows and its longitudinal movement has lessened from the speed it had achieved while transiting the early degrees of Aries and Libra.

The following table of the Sun's simultaneous movement by longitude and declination will demonstrate these points. You will have already recognized the positions referred to as the spring and fall equinoxes and the summer and winter solstices. At the summer and winter solstices the Sun at 0 Cancer + or 0 Capricorn + activates its own solstice points at 29 Gemini + and 29 Sagittarius + while forming an out of sign conjunction with those Points; at the equinoxes the Sun at 0 Aries + and 0 Libra + activates its Solstice Points at 29 Virgo + and 29 Pisces + while forming an out of sign opposition to them. There is every reason to assume that the Sun in positions described above will exercise a tremendous amount of energy and influence, as will any planet in those positions as long as that planet occupies the same degree of declination that the Sun occupies in that position (0N/S + minutes and 23N/S28).

Fixed sign planets and their fixed sign solstice points in the middle degrees of Taurus, Leo, Scorpio, and Aquarius can be simultaneously subject to a parallel conjunction and a parallel square to its own solstice point. This is awesome in its implications. For example:

Sun, 14 Taurus 30, 16N12

Solstice point, 15 Leo 30, 16N12

In this position the Sun is square its own solstice point by longitude and conjunction its own solstice point by parallel of declination.

Consider the influence of a progressed or transiting planet on a natal planet in the middle degrees of any of the fixed signs:

Activating planet at 13, 14, 15 Scorpio, 15, 16, 17S declination will parallel oppose and longitudinally square the Leo solstice point while in both parallel opposition and longitudinal opposition to the natal planet at 14, 15, 16 Taurus.

Activating planet at 13, 14, 15 Aquarius, 15, 16, 17N declination will parallel and oppose the Leo solstice point while making a parallel opposition and a longitudinal square to the natal planet 14 Taurus.

Activating planet at 13, 14, 15 Leo, 15, 16, 17N declination will parallel conjunction the Leo solstice point while parallel conjunction and longitudinally square to the natal planet 14 Taurus.

Activating planet at 13, 14, 15 Taurus, 15, 16, 17N declination will parallel conjunction the Leo solstice point while longitudinally conjunction natal planet 14 Taurus.

Such action in fixed signs is critical and promises that related matters will surely come to pass and can not be avoided.

Solstice points initiate changes; a change of season; a change of conditions; a turning point, a critical time or event.

The table on the following page allows us to see how the Sun gains and loses momentum as it moves through its orbit.

Table of Solar Movement by Longitude and Declination

Sun's longitude noon GMT		Sun's declination noon GMT	
3/21/1992	0 Ar 07:23	0N26:50	
3/25/1992	5 Ar 05:23	2N01:21	
movement	4 d 58:00	movement 1d34:31	
5/3/1992	13 Ta 07:50	-14N42:18	
5/7/1992	17 Ta 10:19	15N49:51	
movement	4 d 02:29	movement 1:05:43	
6/21/1992	-0 Ca 20:51	23N26:23	
6/25:1992	4 Ca 09:48	-23N22:29	
movement	3 d 48:57	movement 00:56:06	

Other concentrations of energy occur at the time and place of eclipses and of lunations and of the lunar and planetary nodes; *all* occur *on* the Ecliptic and *in* degrees of corresponding longitude and declination that define the *time* and *place* along the ecliptic. Of all the astrological indicators in the chart, only the celestial bodies that have form, substance, and independent orbits of their own can establish their position by declination independent of the ecliptic. Their longitudinal position will *always* be found along the ecliptic while their declination can place them far from the ecliptic. When this happens it is imperative, particularly in the case of out-of-bounds planets, to find a corresponding degree of declination that will tie them to the ecliptic by declination. This degree of declination will then be identified with its degree of longitude along the ecliptic.

Arabian Parts, midpoints, house cusps, pre-natal, progressed and transiting eclipses, lunations, nodes, and solstice points exercise their influence exclusively *on* the ecliptic in the degree and minute of declination which the Sun has, so to speak "married" to the degree and minute of longitude in which they are found. In a correctly timed chart, the house cusps, Arabian Parts, midpoints, eclipses, lunations, and lunar nodes are the most reliable timers and indicators of action and its nature because they are inherently incapable of existing and functioning anywhere but on the ecliptic, where the action will take place.

Planets and asteroids that have independent orbits of their own are found in longitudinal degrees that have no relationship along the ecliptic with the degree of declination that they have achieved and thus cannot be so dependable in guaranteeing events and timing of events. Their complete influence in a chart can be concealed in part or in whole if only their longitude is considered. These facts constitute two excellent reasons why these planets and asteroids *must* be associated by their declination with its matching sign and degree of longitude on the ecliptic.

The problem with this has always been an inability to deal with the two different types of data base; to draw cogent information from declination and incorporate that with the obvious and easily recognized information derived from longitude.

The charts included in this study will demonstrate how important it may be to have the ability to convert degrees of declination into the degrees of longitude.

Out-of-Bounds Ceres and Childbirth

The key activator in this chart example is the out-of-bounds asteroid Ceres whose extreme declination signals frantically for special attention by means of its extreme declination far outside the boundary of normality established by the ecliptic. Ceres is the asteroid identified as the legal wife, maternal principle and process (including pregnancy), the mother, and those matters associated with childbearing and the care and mothering of children.

Out-of-bounds planets or asteroids are celestial bodies that have exceeded the maximum declination of the ecliptic as defined by the Sun at 23N/S28 declination; they warn of conditions and/or events that are beyond normal human experience and/or comprehension and are related to those matters associated with or ruled by that particular out-of-bounds celestial body. If you have an out-of-bounds planet or asteroid in your chart, start looking for its hidden and important message. You need to know!

In this instance natal Ceres, representing the legal wife, the maternal principal, i.e., related to the birth of children in this woman's natal chart partile conjunction her fourth cusp and making a partile trine to the Sun, ruler of the maternal tenth cusp and a near partile quintile to Jupiter, (ruler of the third house of congenital or inherited conditions and co-ruler of the fifth cusp of children), warns us of unusual conditions due to a congenital condition inherited from the maternal forebears that will make itself known during pregnancy and childbirth. Her natal uncorrected Ceres makes no significant aspects in the husband's chart. This is quite unusual since the wife's natal Ceres most often makes an important aspect in the husband's natal chart. This is another clue that it is necessary to sort out this problem. Sometimes what doesn't happen in a chart that should happen is simply hidden in declination.

With Ceres at 0 Aquarius 40 (0 degrees are critical) and 31S01, it is imperative to search for the hidden message and we do this by first determining the ecliptic degree of declination with which 31S01 is aligned with thus activating that degree of declination and its associated longitude along the path of the ecliptic:

Natal Ceres: 0 Aquarius 40, 31S01

	31S01 declination of natal Ceres
minus	-23S28 maximum declination of the ecliptic
difference	- 7:33 to minus from ecliptic max. dec.
equals	15S55 whose longitudinal degree may then be

found by referring to the Longitude/Declination Conversion Table. If greater exactitude is desired, refer to any ephemeris and find the Sun at 15S55 declination in the sign of Aquarius. This will give a co-longitudinal position at or close to 16 Aquarius forming a square to natal Jupiter at 17 Scorpio 24 and a parallel conjunction with natal Jupiter (Jupiter at 16S15 declination parallel conjunction Ceres at 15S55 declination). Here we have the exact complex of aspects described in a preceding chapter warning that this particular combination of aspects and solstice points holds inherent threats that cannot be avoided and will be critical. What cannot be cured must be endured.

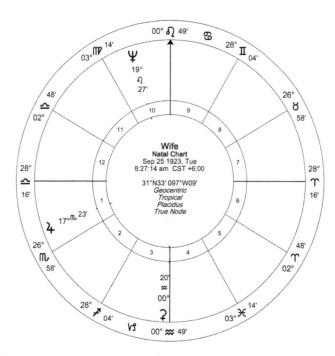

O-O-B Ceres 0 Aquarius, 31S01
Declination and co-declination Ceres
15S55, 16 Aquarius, 14 Scorpio
Jupiter, 16S15
Neptune 15S12

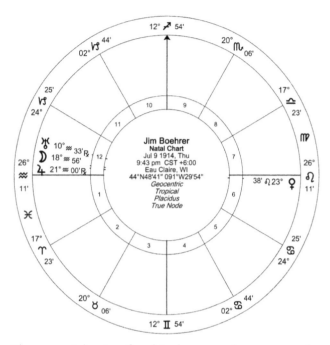

Jim Boehrer
Natal Chart
Jul 9 1914, Thu
9:43 pm CST +6:00
Eau Claire, WI
44°N48'41" 091°W29'54"
Geocentric
Tropical
Placidus
True Node

The potential exists for this danger to become greatly en-
hanced if the native marries a man whose chart has important
placements at 0, 14, 15, or 16 degrees of any fixed sign or at
15N55 or 15S55 declination.

The husband's chart reveals the strong affinity between these
two people and emphasizes the potential in the wife's natal chart
with two planets, the Moon at 16S39 and Jupiter at 15S21, parallel conjunction the wife's natal codeclination Ceres at 15S55,
and two other planets, Venus at 15N13 and Mercury at 16N43
parallel opposition the wife's natal Ceres.

On the day of their marriage (August 19, 1943) the South
Node (long lasting ties and associations) was at 15 Aquarius 53,
16S05 declination parallel conjunction her natal co-declination/
co-longitude Ceres and parallel conjunction his natal Moon and
Jupiter.

On November 15, 1943, the birth date of the first child, the Moon transiting in Scorpio made a parallel square to all the father's Aquarius planets and to the mother's co-declination/co-longitudinal Ceres while simultaneously forming a conjunction to each of their solstice points. The mother's life was endangered and she was very ill but recovered satisfactorily.

June 3, 1947, the birth date of the second child, Venus at 17 Taurus 15N40 and Jupiter at 20 Scorpio 16S42 aspected all the planets listed above with parallel squares, parallel oppositions, and parallel conjunctions to the parents' planets in Aquarius, Scorpio, and Leo, and the mother's co-declination/co-longitude Ceres. Because of the benign nature of Venus and Jupiter the complications were far less severe.

The birth of the third child was the most critical of all. The mother was pronounced dead and a Caesarian operation was performed without benefit of anaesthetic (a body with no vital signs cannot be anesthetized) in what proved to be a successful attempt to save the child.

On that day, May 11, 1956, surgical Mars at 16 Aquarius 41 made a partile conjunction to the mother's natal co-longitudinal Ceres and a close conjunction with all the father's Aquarius planets. Mars' declination that day at 17S39 made myriad parallel aspects to the square and solstice points of the mother's out-of-bounds Ceres and the father's natal Aquarius planets and co-declination Leo planets. Both mother and child were pronounced dead but miraculously survived.

All three of these children were healthy and normal children from birth. Even the third child who did not breathe for an hour after delivery began a vigorous and active life in a rather miraculous fashion with his first breath.

The only physiological incompatibility ever identified with the parents came to light just one year after the birth of the first child with discovery of the Rh factor; the mother was Rh negative while the father was Rh positive. Curiously, the mother, during the first pregnancy, developed an inexplicable anaemia of pregnancy and was given nine blood transfusions of which three caused extreme reactions that were nearly deadly. The donors of those three transfusions were identified a year later as Rh positive.

Each birth involved different and totally unrelated problems that could not be scientifically or medically anticipated, explained or accounted for. The only problems that could be associated with the Rh factor were those resulting from the three Rh positive transfusions.

The prophecy of the natal chart was fulfilled.

Out-of-Bounds Planets and Abnormal Psychology

I have researched the mental, physical, emotional, and spiritual impact of the out-of-bounds planets on humanity. This article addresses the mental and emotional health of a limited number of diagnosed schizophrenics, some of whom committed violent crimes.

Planets found on either the maximum ecliptic declination or on the minimum declination (0N/S00 plus or minus a degree) are of enormous import in any chart and deserving of special consideration. Because the significance of planets found at 0N/S00 has long been recognized by astrologers, attention throughout this research has been focused on the out-of-bounds planets whose importance had gone unrecognized throughout the history of astrology.

I would also like to acknowledge my indebtedness to Harry F. Darling, M.D. for the thirty-one birth charts used in this research.

Out-of-bounds planets are not an everyday phenomenon. For example, the Moon is out of bounds only about one-fifth of the time. These out-of-bounds periods occur every other decade (give or take a few months). During this ten-year period she will be found out of bounds approximately two to twelve days per month, for an average of up to 144 days per year. These out-of-bounds days occur at intervals of about eight to twelve days throughout the ten-year out-of-bounds period; the Moon is thus out of bounds only a few days at a time each time that the phenomenon occurs. The ten-year out-of-bounds cycle alternates with another ten- year cycle (actually closer to a nine-year cycle) during which the Moon never goes out of bounds. Taking both of these periods as the complete cycle for the Moon we can arrive at a figure for the Moon's out-of-bounds condition as being in effect roughly one-fifth of the time; we can thus expect that in any nineteen-year period no more than about one-fifth of the people born will have an out-of-bounds Moon (and it may be less than that since the birth rate is not evenly distributed in time).

Of the remaining planets, two, Saturn and Neptune (reality and illusion) never exceed the ecliptic limits—a very practical arrangement!

Venus is found out of bounds from one to three times a year for periods of from one day to sixty days. Mercury is out of bounds two or three times a year for periods of one day to about one month. Mars goes out of bounds once a year for one day up to two and a half months. Jupiter goes out of bounds approximately every six years for a period of approximately six to nine weeks, while Uranus' out-of-bounds cycle happens about every forty years and lasts off and on for about four years. Pluto goes out of bounds approximately every 140 years and is then found out of bounds intermittently for approximately fifteen years as far as I am able to determine. However, I must beg you not to hold me to the figures given for erratic Pluto, whose cycle I have researched for only a few hundred years, and with Pluto, who can say what he may be doing when we're not looking!

Research over the past twenty-odd years strongly indicates

that out-of-bounds planets exercise an extremely important influence over individuals. In this particular study we wish to determine if there is reasonable cause to associate out-of-bounds planets with mental and emotional illness and extremes of behavior.

It is my profound conviction that the natal chart reveals the DNA pattern of the native and that the condition of the planets (by sign, house, aspects, dignity, debility, fall, exaltation, and out of bounds condition) and their relation to the chart as a whole will some day be seen to contain all information relative to the physical makeup—the chemical composition of the native, from whence spring all actions. Medical research and treatment today goes a long way toward confirmation of the hypothesis that our moods, attitudes, and actions all result from the chemical composition of our physical bodies. Tranquilizers, mood elevators, etc., are the first rather clumsy attempts of science to relieve chemical imbalance that creates mental and emotional illness.

Psychiatry relies more and more on medication and less and less on psychotherapy as time goes by and of course the implication of this is that the scientific world is becoming daily more convinced that mental illness is a true physical malfunction and the disordered mind and emotion are no more than the symptom or result.

Given the hypothesis that the natal planets reveal the chemical character of the native, the most striking feature of the chart with one or more planets out of bounds is the tremendous energy demonstrated in the individual. We find that those born with natal out-of-bounds planets are high achievers, even overachievers. They are people who rise from obscurity to positions of dignity, fame, or power. They are the rags-to-riches, Cinderella/Horatio Alger types who make their mark on the world through their own efforts. They expend a tremendous amount of energy in reaching their goal. They achieve prominence, if not more often than we ordinary mortals with all planets within the ecliptic limits, certainly against greater odds. This is not to say that all our high achievers are limited to those born with natal out-of-bounds planets; Mother Nature through astrology, has more than one way of producing the same result. Nevertheless, it is a striking fact that research indicates that a disproportionate number of these remarkable people have out-of-bounds planets in their natal charts and we may well conclude that these out-of-bounds planets represent a chemical composition that produces great energy which, when applied constructively, can carry the native to the heights.

The other side of the coin, naturally, is the realization that this tremendous energy can become uncontrollable or be misused. In such cases the potential for destructive action is devastating and the contrasting potential of the out-of-bounds planets would seem to prove that "genius hovers on the edge of madness" is, in fact, a great truth.

Theoretically, planets represent the chemical composition that produces the energies available for our use during our lifetime. Out-of-bounds planets produce (or symbolize the production) of extraordinary energy that may be used either constructively or destructively or, in some cases, can become uncontrollable.

If this theory is correct we should find an extraordinary number of out-of-bounds planets in the charts of mentally ill persons. One of the most disturbing features of mental illness is the fearful amount of energy displayed, including an inability to sleep, even under sedation, for long periods of time. When the subject finally falls asleep it is most often of brief duration and characterized by restlessness of the physical body and of the mind. The subject most often dreams constantly—violent, active dreams accompanied by verbal expressions of the mental activity even while the dream is occurring.

I have in my files the chart of a young man whose diagnosis was paranoid schizophrenia. He was released from the hospital while still acutely ill and within two weeks after being sent home he shot and killed a member of the family. The surviving members of the family stated that at least one member of the family had to stay awake and alert at all times; the patient exhibited great mental, emotional, and physical energy, rarely sleeping and thus posing a constant problem to other members of the family who required a normal amount of rest, relaxation and sleep.

There is, of course, the catatonic state in which the patient becomes as still as a wax figure; do not be deceived by this. The catatonic patient is not at rest; he or she is, in fact, expending a considerable amount of energy in maintaining a catatonic state.

One other factor should be taken into consideration: in any random group of charts that pass through my hands I normally find out-of-bounds planets in no more than about thirty-five percent of the total number. The chart data assembled by Dr. Darling is random in that it covers a period of time from 1893 through 1957. On the other hand, it is specific because every birth date given is that of a diagnosed schizophrenic.

The first step was to determine how many of these charts contained out-of-bounds planets. Of the thirty-one charts, twenty had one or more out-of-bounds planets. This is nearly sixty-six percent, a much greater proportion of out-of-bounds planets than should be anticipated in any random sampling of birth dates. This must certainly be considered, at the very least, remarkably strong support of the theory advanced in this paper.

The twenty charts exhibiting out-of-bounds planets are listed below:

November 11, 1893, 9:44 GMT; Moon, 27S 41; Mercury, 24S43; Venus, 26S13

December 13, 1943, 9:30 GMT; Mercury, 25S30; Mars, 24N16

February 14, 1911, 14:59 GMT; Mars, 23S27

July 14, 1912, 21:30 GMT; Moon, 25N36

October 1, 1920, 12:00 GMT; Mars, 24S39

January 31, 1929, 28:23 GMT; Mars, 26N23

December 8, 1929, 8:43 GMT; Mercury, 24S51

October 29, 1935, 15:50 GMT; Moon, 23S47; Mars, 24S56

August 21, 1937, 14:27 GMT; Mars, 23S56

March 18, 1940, 15:44 GMT; Pluto, 23N47

July 1, 1942, 7:15 GMT; Pluto, 23N39

March 25, 1945, 6:38 GMT; Pluto, 24N04

December 20, 1946, 8:14 GMT; Mars, 24S13

January 14, 1949, 17:01 GMT; Moon, 26N36; Uranus, 23N37; Pluto, 23N31

March 7, 1949, 12:25 GMT; Moon, 25N38; Uranus, 23N36; Pluto, 23N56

November 29, 1949, 6:35 GMT; Venus, 24S19; Uranus, 23N38

March 23, 1950, 17:15 GMT; Moon, 23N41; Uranus, 23N42; Pluto, 23N55

August 12, 1954, 13:10 GMT, Mars, 28S05

June 2, 1956, 16:30 GMT; Venus, 25N10

The out-of-bounds planets break down thusly:

- 6 charts with Mars alone out of bounds
- 2 charts with Venus alone out of bounds
- 2 charts with Pluto alone out of bounds
- 1 chart with Moon alone out of bounds
- 1 chart with Mercury alone out of bounds
- No charts with either Jupiter or Uranus alone out of bounds
- No charts with Jupiter out of bounds
- 8 charts with combinations of out-of-bounds planets
- Mars out of bounds in 8 charts
- Pluto out of bounds in 7 charts
- Venus out of bounds in 5 charts

- Uranus out of bounds in 4 charts
- Moon and Mercury out of bounds in 3 charts

Of the eleven charts showing no natal planets out of bounds I expect that progressed and transiting out of bounds planets play a large part in the onset and progress of the condition. For example, one of the eleven charts having no out-of-bounds planets is that of Richard Speck. Yet I note that by July 13, 1966, when Speck murdered eight women, his progressed Mercury and progressed Pluto were out of bounds, Mercury at 24S55. The day of the terrible massacre transiting Mars was at 24N01 declination, out of bounds and forming a parallel opposition to progressed Mercury, which, incidentally, or perhaps not so incidentally, rules Speck's natal Ascendant.

The chart of the beautiful, gifted, and gentle Vivian Leigh, who was a diagnosed schizophrenic manic depressive, is one of the twenty charts in which we find out-of-bounds planets. Born with natal Mercury out of bounds, she suffered her first serious attack of mental illness in 1952, when her progressed Moon was out of bounds at 28N18 (just about as far out as a planet can go) and progressed Mars was out of bounds at 24N43. Obviously, we are affected by progressed and transiting out-of-bounds planets as well as natal out-of-bounds planets.

Because out-of-bounds planets are so consistently involved in unexpected, uncommon matters and conditions, their key phrase is "beyond normal expectations." It pays to watch them closely!

Chapter 3

Out-of-Bounds Examples

The following stories illustrate the out-of-bounds Moon at work.

The Cat Burglar Goes Out of Bounds

Frank Hohimer, cat burglar, was more elusive and frustrating to police than any criminal in the nation. His fabulous career earned him $3 to $5 million a year. Men like him seldom reach age forty; they are either killed by police or by their employer, organized crime. He was a rebel like many brilliant men. He used his brilliance, however, in rebelling against the laws of that society in a quest for the immediate rewards his age demanded. He wanted flashy clothes, fast cars, and the power of money, but he did not have the patience or maturity to wait. To study his chart is to look into the workings of an ingenious and devious mind. For him, life was filled with dangerous and daring events; but certainly the most unusual and sensational was his jailbreak, which was timed by a transiting out-of-bounds Moon.

The Home Invaders: Confessions of a Cat Burglar was written in 1974 by Frank Hohimer while doing time in a midwestern prison. The event that put him on the F.B.I. most wanted list was the smoothest escape ever pulled off from the correctional center in Bridgeport, Connecticut. The circumstances leading up to the jailbreak, which took place in the first week of July 1971, are given in the following brief appraisal of his natal chart:

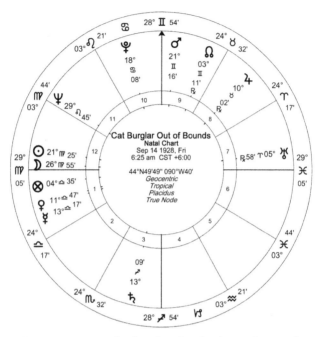

Hohimer was one of a family of eight, born during the Depression to uneducated, underprivileged parents. Saturn in the third house shows limitation and sorrow in his early home environment. He had to fend for himself at an early age. 29 Sagittarius on the fourth house cusp is in a Leo decanate and is trine Neptune at 29 Leo in the eleventh house (wishes and circumstances beyond his control), showing his dreams for a home and background to be proud of.

To compensate for this lack of prestige, he bought big cars, expensive clothes, and traveled first class. Limiting Saturn in freedom-loving Sagittarius in the third house denied him a formal education. However, Venus in the first house, and as the chart's final dispositor, gave protection and compensation. So, although denied education by a third house Saturn, Venus conjunction Mercury, ruler of the Ascendant, made him extremely street wise. Natal Mercury sextile Saturn shows gain through special education in later life. The Sun in the twelfth house of self-undoing and bondage, square Mars of unrestrained action in the ninth house of the higher courts, indicates the eleven years spent in prison for a crime he did not commit.

In prison, Hohimer learned three trades: barbering, Mars in Gemini conjunction Midheaven), music (Venus in Libra, Neptune in Leo), and cat burglary. Venus and Mercury square Pluto in Cancer, intercepted in the tenth house, indicates a career connected with home invasion and leadership of a gang of professional burglars. Jupiter in the eighth house sextile Pluto gives penetrating insight for making money through underworld activities. He was taught the profession by the best, a man never caught for burglary but for murder. Hohimer learned his lessons well, shown by Saturn trine Uranus, from the third house of learning to the seventh of partners.

Frank Hohimer began his life as a cat burglar after his release from an Illinois state prison in 1962. He bought several barber shops and used them successfully as fronts for his burglary activities, Neptune trine Midheaven and Jupiter in Taurus (the Midas touch), in a behind-the-scenes position to the ninth house of legal activities and law.

During this time he became involved with organized crime, an association he was later to regret. He found that once he was in, the only way out was by death. In an attempt to leave the mob, Hohimer began drawing public attention to himself as an underworld character (Moon square Mars), hoping by doing this, he would no longer be useful to them and, thereby, eased out. In the chart this is shown by a 29-degree Vertex (a fated point, in Pisces of self-undoing), conjunction the seventh house cusp of partners and open enemies in a quincunx, readjustment aspect, to Neptune in the eleventh house of circumstances out of his control.

His plans failed and he dropped out of sight in 1967 and opened a very successful pancake house in Connecticut.

It was while running this pancake house in Cos Cob, that the F.B.I. arrested him on what he claimed were false charges. His natal yod, indicating this destiny-fulfilling event, was activated on December 20, 1969, by an out-of-bounds Mercury, ruling the first, tenth, and twelfth houses. The planets involved in the yod were Jupiter, at the action point in the eighth, quincunx Venus and Mercury in the first, and Saturn in the third. The co-declination degree of Mercury was 19 Sagittarius to conjunct Saturn and activate the yod.

He was sent to the Bridgeport Correctional Center (Sun sextile Pluto), and placed under maximum security, pending the outcome of an appeal to the state supreme court (Neptune in the eleventh house square Lilith in the second), on a plea of illegal arrest to avoid extradition to Denver for a $50,000 jewel theft. After a two-year delay (Jupiter retrograde), when his appeal was denied, Hohimer decided to escape with the aid of an eastern crime family (Mars sextile Neptune, planet of escape, at the end-of-the-rope 29 degrees).

The necessary contacts were made and an agent was planted in the prison to make the arrangements. The agent informed Hohimer on June 30, 1971 (transiting Mercury, ruling agents, was out of bounds at 18 Cancer conjunction Pluto, ruling the underworld in the tenth house of fate), that the mob would provide a getaway car, which should be stationed outside the prison gate on July 3, 4, and 5. He was told he would have to take care of the inside details himself.

The events leading up to his escape can be shown by following the secondary progressed and directed planets from July 1 to 11 and transits of an out-of-bounds Moon. These events reveal changes in the life of Frank Hohimer that were to be far beyond the norm.

On July 1, Mercury, by secondary progression, made a trine to the lunation midpoint in the ninth house of legal documents. Mars (locks) at 21 Aquarius (freedom) was in transit in the natal fifth house of risks, and made a partile trine to its natal position in the ninth house.

Hohimer made his way to the front office, where he stole and destroyed his photos and bond papers. The Moon in transit was parallel secondary progressed Mercury, which was an aid to him in finding his records. Transiting Mercury was still out of bounds on July 1 and had just left a conjunction to Pluto (erasures) for the destruction of his photo, warrant, and bond.

On July 2, Hohimer managed to get his remaining records, F.B.I. reports, and fingerprint cards from a locked cabinet and destroy them.

Protective Venus, by transit, was at 24 Gemini (records) square the solstice point of Uranus in Virgo in the twelfth house (locks and closets). Transiting Mercury was sextile the natal Sun in the twelfth house (confidential matters).

On July 3, the secondary progressed Moon at 11 Aries in the seventh house (open enemies) made a square to the Part of Captivity and Escape at 11 Cancer in his tenth house (destiny).

In order to make his escape after the night count, Hohimer needed a device to unlock his cell. During the day he took a spoon (Mercury) and made a key from it. Mars (tools), planet of action, was out of bounds by secondary progression at 7 Cancer to square the solstice point of the Sun (authority) in the seventh house (law and open enemies) and also in conjunction with its own solstice point in the tenth house (fate).

He stole a wire coat hanger and fashioned a tool for picking locks (Mars).

On July 4, the day planned for his escape, the Sun at 11 Cancer moved by transit into interception to conjunct the Part of Captivity and Escape in the tenth house. Transiting Mercury (decisions) at 26 Cancer also went into interception, indicating a delay. The Moon at 23 Scorpio, 23S40 declination, out-of-bounds by 13 minutes, moved to a conjunction of Lilith in his second house of the immediate future, again to delay his plans. Seeing there was too much activity in the front office, he postponed his escape to the following day.

On July 5, the Moon at 13 Sagittarius (freedom) made a partile conjunction to Saturn (plans) in his third house of travel.

Hohimer's plans were now working like a clock.

The declination of the Moon was 26S09, moving further out of bounds.

He was ready to make his break. There was only one man on duty in the front office.

By solar arc direction, Mars at 3 Leo made a trine to the solstice point of the natal Moon in the seventh house of open enemies.

At the 8:00 count he left right behind the guards to walk from the north cell house to a side gate where he used his "spoon" key and his wire coat hanger to gain access to the front office. He ran into no real trouble because Venus the Protector, his chart's final dispositor, was transiting the lunation midpoint, 28 Gemini, and the Midheaven. Mercury, his life ruler, by solar arc direction was now conjunct Lilith (back street sphere of action) in his second house and sextile (opportunity) his natal Moon in the twelfth house of prisons.

Transiting Mercury, ruling his natal twelfth and first houses, moved to 29 Cancer and made a trine to the vertex (fated point) at 29 Pisces, on his seventh cusp, activating all the angles.

It is unusual for the Vertex to be exactly on the Descendant, as in this chart.

His next moves to make his escape (Pisces) would depend upon the guards staying with their normal routine.

The Moon's declination, 23S46, was now out-of-bounds by 2 degrees 42 minutes and its co-declination points were 29 Scorpio 50 and 0 Aquarius 08, both critical degrees.

Hohimer couldn't turn back. He had to make it. He was at the door of the front office.

The longitudinal position of the Moon, 13 Sagittarius, made a partile conjunction to Saturn (doors) and a partile sextile to Mercury (offices). Transiting Mars was at 21 Aquarius inconjunct his natal Sun at 21 Virgo in the twelfth house.

He dropped to the floor and crawled back of the counter, to the warden's door while the guard's back was turned. He put the flat end of the coat hanger (Mars in Aquarius) into the lock, carefully opened the door and crawled through.

The Moon at the co-declination point, 29 Scorpio, made a partile square (difficulties) to Neptune in Leo (risks) in his eleventh house of hopes and wishes).

He was in the warden's office where he saw a sliding canvas door behind the drapes. It opened into the counselor's office. He tried the windows but they were locked tight with paint (Neptune). He could see the car waiting for him. Realizing the windows were his only way out, he pulled until the paint broke loose. He climbed through the window and ran, undetected, across the well lighted prison yard to the waiting car.

The Moon's co-declination point, 29 Scorpio, made an inconjunct, readjustment aspect to the Midheaven of fate. The transiting Moon in Sagittarius (freedom and distant travel) was moving further out-of-bounds. He was free!

He was driven to New York, where he met with one of the mob's members, who scheduled a meeting for the following Monday, July 12, to make the final arrangements for the heist (which he was to make for them as the price of his escape). Later, Hohimer checked into a hotel. He wanted to call his wife to let her know he was free. She was unaware of his escape for he had not revealed his plans, fearing she would prove to be a hindrance and, too, he wished to protect her. He put off calling her until the following day.

Transiting Venus at 29 Gemini was conjunct the Midheaven and square (obstacle) the first and seventh (mate) cusps.

On July 6, at noon, the Moon was 19 Sagittarius and had moved to its greatest distance beyond the ecliptic, 27S17. Venus, his life co-ruler, reached 29 Gemini to conjunct his Midheaven (news and publicity). His escape had finally reached the media. By evening, Mercury, life ruler, made a sextile (opportunity) to his Ascendant, 29 Virgo, and trine aspect to the seventh cusp (partners). He contacted his wife and made arrangements to meet her the following day.

On July 7, the Moon was still out of bounds, 26S54, but was now decreasing. His life co-ruler, Venus, at the critical 0 Cancer, made a separative inconjunct aspect to transiting Neptune at 0 Sagittarius. After a long talk with his wife he was convinced that he should stop running and give himself up. The F.B.I. was hot on his trail and he was under the pressure of the mob. Mercury (decisions) by solar arc was 25 Scorpio, conjunction Lilith, the dark moon planet of daring trickery, ambush and deceit. If the F.B.I. caught up with him the worst they could do was put him in jail. On the other hand, if the mob should find him first he'd be murdered for double-crossing them.

On July 8, Uranus, the planet ruling unexpected events, had progressed to 18 Taurus by solar arc to make a sextile to Pluto in his tenth house of fate (bargaining and the F.B.I.).

The Full Moon (a culmination of events) was still out of bounds, 24S54, but decreasing in declination. It was conjunct the solstice point of Saturn in the fourth house of endings. This was a turning point for Hohimer. He had decided to give himself up to the F.B.I. in exchange for putting himself in their custody and avoiding extradition to Denver; he offered information on the mob leaders.

On July 9, the Moon entered 0 Aquarius 19, and on July 9 returned to a position within the ecliptic (21S21 declination).

The deal was made. He agreed to turn himself in on Sunday, July 11, at midnight. He spent Saturday and Sunday with his wife and child.

It is interesting to note that Hohimer made his escape when the Moon's longitude was 29 Scorpio and out of bounds. He gave himself up in a final arrangement with the F.B.I. when the Moon returned to the ecliptic at 0 Aquarius, the same position as the co-declination position on July 5.

On July 11, the transiting Sun of authority was 18 Cancer conjunction natal Pluto in his tenth of destiny. He arrived at the F.B.I. office around midnight when transiting Mercury in Leo made a trine aspect to the solstice point of the Sun in the seventh house of justice.

Hohimer was turned over to the U.S. attorney general and the Chicago Strike Force on Organized Crime.

The race had been run and time was up for Frank Hohimer. The Moon had run its course out-of-bounds and back to the ecliptic. From the widest point of south latitude, five degrees, to the lowest point, 0S00, on July 11. It timed every significant change taking place from July 1 to 11.

The Out-of-Bounds Moon and Surgery

The following letter was received:

"Enclosed is my birth chart. I have had many serious problems with my health, all of which have developed since the birth of my last child on September 28, 1958.

"My birth data is December 29, 1933, 5:23:14 a.m. CST, 40N00, 86W00.

"History of illness: Cancerous tumors removed from breasts in February 1961 and January 1962. Cancerous tumor of the uterus removed January 1969. This tumor had developed very rapidly (three months time).

"Phlebitis and resultant surgery (veins stripped) in February 1972.

"No one has been able to find any real health problems in my chart."

Our response:

"It is rather surprising that astrologers have been unable to find in your chart the physical problems that you have outlined. The indications of your surgeries are as clearly defined for the astrologer to read as the medical tests and physical symptoms are for your doctors. Perhaps even more clearly defined, in fact, for the astrologer."

The first warning is found in the out-of-bounds Moon at 26N54 declination. The Moon ruling the eighth cusp of surgery is the second warning and the Moon's corrected declination to 20N02 giving a co-declination position at 29 Taurus 35 (the weeping degree, something to cry about) and 0 Leo 35 is (0 degrees 00 any sign is always critical). These indications are clearly red alerts, warnings of extremely serious surgery, probably involving the breasts (ruled by the Moon) and the female reproductive organs. Other organs that serve as containers in the body are also associated with the Moon.

Natal Mercury is also out of bounds at 23S46 and in Sagittarius, which is associated with veins and the circulation of the blood. Mercury's corrected declination position at 23S10 does not take it out of Sagittarius and since Mercury rules miniaturization, Mercury in Sagittarius may represent very narrow veins and constricted circulation.

Although there are no exact dates of surgery provided, an examination of the planets' declination during February 1961 shows surgical Mars out of bounds at 27N02 parallel the out-of-bounds natal Moon at 26N54 from the first day of February through the 28th day for the removal of tumors of the breasts during that month.

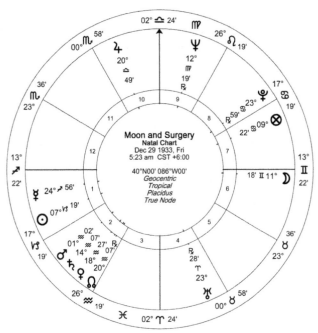

Moon and Surgery
Natal Chart
Dec 29 1933, Fri
5:23 am CST +6:00

40°N00' 086°W00'
Geocentric
Tropical
Placidus
True Node

At the time of the second breast surgery, Mars was again out of bounds from January 1, 1962 through January 13, 1962. Mercury was also out of bounds from January 1-3, 1962 for a repeat performance.

Surgery was performed to remove the cancerous tumor of the uterus in January 1969. During that month the Moon was out of bounds January 1-3, 14-18, and 27-31.

The veins were stripped in February 1972 and we find the Moon out of bounds February 8-11 and 21-24.

The odds are very great that all of the surgeries were performed during the out of bounds periods listed.

The natal chart is replete with indications of the nature of the health problems but the out-of-bounds Moon and Mercury sum them up very clearly and easily so that even a beginner astrologer might diagnose the health problems of this chart.

The Perilous Journey

On June 17, 1970, three young people embarked by boat on an ocean trip from Bora Bora to Hawaii. What should have been a lovely, carefree voyage became a nightmare and almost cost them their lives.

The first week out of port the weather was so choppy that they were seasick and unable to eat. In the long run (and it was a long run) this was a blessing and probably saved their lives.

On June 29, the boat's starter motor broke and they could not repair it because of its inaccessibility. From that point they had to rely on sails. Within two days they found themselves in the Doldrums at the equator and were literally immobilized for several days.

Finally, the winds came up again but unfortunately they had problems using the sextant and could only estimate where they might be. Their radio went out. They were forced to use rather primitive methods of navigation.

Their food and water supplies had given out by this time and they were desperate. After eating everything edible they finally ate the potted rhododendron and were forced to scrape the algae off the side of the boat and eat a kind of soup they made of it. Their fishing tackle was worthless and they could not bring a fish in with it.

After that they encountered a ship one night that refused to acknowledge them although they had rigged a bonfire that hung out over the water and fired guns to attract attention.

By the beginning of September they were nearly dead, and much of their time was spent in endless hallucinations, many having to do with food that they could see, smell, and almost eat.

On the morning of September 14, 1970, they heard a clattering sound and dragged themselves to the deck where they discovered that the noise was being made by a small boat be-

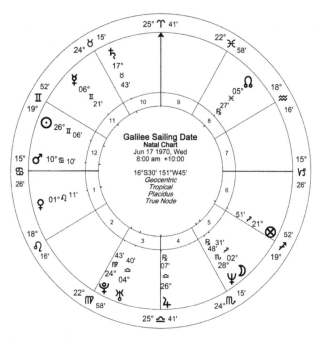

Galilee Sailing Date
Natal Chart
Jun 17 1970, Wed
8:00 am +10:00

16°S30' 151°W45'
Geocentric
Tropical
Placidus
True Node

ing launched from a huge grey ship, the U.S.S. Niagara Falls. Within minutes United States sailors were on board and they were rescued.

The Niagara's ship's log registered the exact time and location of the rescue: September 14, 1970, 6:30 a.m., 24N47, 164W42. The navy had landed.

Naval physicians who treated the three adventurers reported that they could not have survived another 24 hours. In fact, they estimated that the young woman who was aboard would not have lived more than another few hours.

The ship had taken the great circle route to Hawaii and the victims were found 455 miles north of Hawaii where there are no sailing lanes, no ocean traffic, nothing!

Was it sheer chance that the U.S.S. Niagara Falls was ordered to take this route?

Is there really such a thing as chance? Accident? Astrology seems to deny that such a factor exists and this story would seem to support the theory. Perhaps there are only miracles!

The boat in which the strange voyage was made carried the name Galilee.

Of all the curious, beyond coincidental connotations that the name brings to mind, one of the most interesting is found in the meaning of the word, for galilee translates as a circle, or circuitous. Certainly the Galilee seemed caught within some unfortunate sphere of influence. Changing course again and again, relentlessly driven, first here, then there, the Galilee and her crew followed their circuitous route, totally unable to break through the watery circle to which they were committed.

What influences were these which trapped this brave boat, sailing with Lady Luck's gallant symbol riding at her prow (Venus in Leo in the first house) within the endless circle? What forces worked mercilessly to crucify the Galilee and her crew upon the cross of the compass points?

The traditional longitudinal chart for the moment of sailing does not tell the whole story. For the complete truth we must always refer to the declination chart and the equivalent longitudinal positions of the planets by declination.

Sailing, as the Galilee did, with the Moon out of bounds is an immediate warning of out-of-the-ordinary events. An out-of-bounds planet is a primary alert signal to the astrologer and dictates an order for investigation of the planet's position by declination.

Although Mars is also found out of bounds at the time of sailing, its declination influence is not so tumultuous. Found by declination at 12 Cancer 02, it is sextile the longitudinal Part of Travel by Water and achieves a closer conjunction with the Ascendant, spelling out an ever-present threat and peril to the Galilee and her crew.

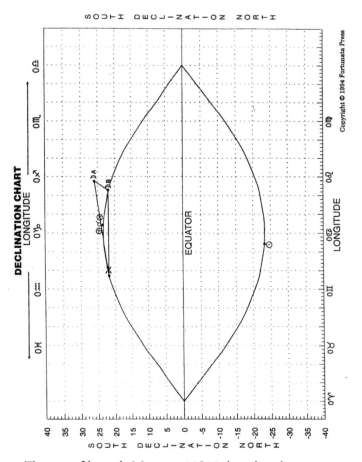

The out-of-bounds Moon at 25S27 describes this ever-present danger, delineating its nature precisely for the astrologer.

You will see by studying the chart given that the Moon's declination position falls at 6 Sagittarius 59, bringing the mutable grand cross formed with Mercury and the lunar nodes to exactitude at the moment of sailing. This is the sacrificial grand cross of the compass within the circle of the Galilee.

In researching the effect of the mutable grand cross I found

Dorothy B. Hughes' delineation most applicable. Ms. Hughes defines the mutable grand cross as a probationary path, a testing, being driven hither and thither, in fact, precisely the nature of the events in which the Galilee became involved.

Further study of the chart reveals yet another cross—the mutable T-cross—set up by the Moon's declination position. We use the Moon's position by declination to find a more exact position for the Part of Fortune, at 26 Sagittarius, bringing this part to partile conjunction with Earth. The Galilee sailed away from land and luck when she embarked upon her watery course (Ascendant in cardinal water). This declination Fortuna conjunction Earth opposed the life-giving Sun at 26 Gemini, and all three (Fortuna, Earth, and the Sun) were balanced by the square on the fulcrum of the declination Part of Death at 26 Virgo (Ascendant plus eighth cusp minus the declination position Moon).

Turn now to the declination chart. The Moon, out of bounds at 25S27, is identified by her symbol and the letter A. Her influence is strongest at letters B (6 Sagittarius 59) and C (23 Capricorn 01). The out-of-bounds degrees are related to the ecliptic and identified by reference to the Declination/Longitude Conversion Table. Letter B locates the Moon's declination position, letter C locates the declination Moon's solstice point, always a turning point in events. The Part of Fortune and Earth are identified and located by the letter D. We have drawn a line from the true declination Moon to connect these points. You will observe that the line from A (the Moon's declination) to C (the turning point of the declination Moon) is precisely bisected (cut in half, blocked) by the declination position of Fortuna and Earth. The Moon, ruler of cardinal water Cancer, peregrine in Sagittarius, was aligned with Earth and Fortuna to set the Galilee and her crew wandering aimlessly on Earth's largest ocean, forever unable to find, through their own efforts, the true turning point in this strange voyage.